ARISTOTLE'S *POETICS*

Phil Zhang
— Haverford
fall 2007

ARISTOTLE'S *POETICS*

Translated, with an Introduction and Notes, by
JAMES HUTTON
LATE OF CORNELL UNIVERSITY

Preface by GORDON M. KIRKWOOD
CORNELL UNIVERSITY

W · W · NORTON & COMPANY · *New York* · *London*

ISBN 0-393-01599-8

ISBN 0-393-95216-9 PBK.

Printed in the United States of America
All Rights Reserved
FIRST EDITION

Library of Congress Cataloging in Publication Data
Aristotle.
  Aristotle's poetics.
  Translation of: Peri poiētikēs.
  1. Poetry—Early works to 1800. 2. Aesthetics—
Early works to 1800. I. Hutton, James, 1902–
II. Title.
PN1040.A513 1982   808.2   81-18815

                    AACR2

W. W. Norton & Company, Inc., 500 Fifth Avenue, New York, N.Y. 10110
www.wwnorton.com

W. W. Norton & Company Ltd., Castle House, 75/76 Wells Street, London W1T 3QT

4567890

Contents

Preface

Although Aristotle's *Poetics* appears to have had little impact on literary criticism in antiquity, critics and scholars since the Renaissance have placed this brief work at the very center of the criticism of poetry and drama. Its prestige began in the sixteenth century, when it was, in James Hutton's words, "Called into life and activity by the needs of Renaissance and modern literature." Since then, in spite of changing fashions in literary criticism, it has held its place firmly as one of the most important guides to the critical reading of drama, especially Greek tragedy. The doctrine of literature as "imitation," the terms "catharsis," "hamartia," and "reversal," the discussion, in Chapter 13, of the types of tragic hero, and many other terms and concepts have become basic materials in the critical discussion not only of tragedy but of narrative and other literary forms. The *Poetics* has permanent importance for the study of literature and for the theory and practice of literary criticism.

The work has often enough been denounced and rejected, and there have always been those who rebel against subjecting their criticism of poetry to a set of Aristotelian "rules." But such rejection is only a symptom of the continuing authority of Aristotle's work, and much of the traditional anti-Aristotelian sentiment (which began with the beginning of its influence, in the Renaissance) is based either on a misunderstanding of what Aristotle in fact *says* in the *Poetics* or, more often, on an application of what he says in ways that are false to Aristotle's spirit and purpose. And that is where Hutton's work in this volume is uniquely important.

Commentators on the *Poetics* have recognized the need to view the *Poetics* in the context of its creation and its re-emergence in the Renaissance. Few, if any, however, have had the combination of talents for this undertaking that were possessed by James Hutton, an accomplished Hellenist with a particularly broad and strong background in the thought of Plato and Aristotle, a graceful stylist in English, and a leading authority on the Renaissance Humanists, who were above all responsible for establishing the prestige of the *Poetics*.

In Hutton's Introduction, readers will find an explanation of the importance and the limitations of the *Poetics*, in terms of Aristotelian thought and its Platonic roots, and in a way that corrects the dogmatism that has often attended the study of the *Poetics*. They will also find a historical outline of the influence of the work on European criticism of poetry and drama.

The translation itself is marked by both accuracy and a refreshing clarity of exposition. It should be observed that the chapter and paragraph headings, which serve the purpose of clarifying Aristotle's sometimes obscure transitions, are added by the translator and are not part of Aristotle's text. The notes provide explication of difficult passages and serve as a glossary for names and terms that occur in the text. The chapters that follow the main body of the *Poetics* are often unjustly slighted. In this volume these chapters—20 through 22 on poetic language, 23 and 24 on epic, and 25 on literary criticism—are carefully and illuminatingly annotated.

This book was complete at the time of James Hutton's death in the fall of 1980, except for minor corrections. I have added a few notes to the Introduction, explaining references and terms that may be unfamiliar to the inexperienced reader. These notes are bracketed and initialed by me. A list of abbreviations has been included (pp. ix-x), in which references made in abbreviated form in the Introduction and in the Notes to the Translation are clarified. A few bibliographical items have been added. Otherwise the volume stands as Hutton left it.

There are some acknowledgments that Hutton would have made if he had lived to see this work through the press. He would have wanted to acknowledge the support of M. H. Abrams, who originally proposed the volume and has cooperated in its progress throughout; he would have expressed his gratitude to Friedrich Solmsen, with whom he discussed the work frequently and in detail; and he would have mentioned the services of Stephen B. Rogers, who was his assistant in the final stages of preparation and who has continued to help in the months since Hutton's death. He would also have wanted to thank John Benedict, of W. W. Norton & Company, for his patience, encouragement, and editorial counsel at all stages of preparation. There may well be others whom he would have named. But all who have been associated with bringing the work to publication find satisfaction in seeing this product of the learning and critical skill of James Hutton completed. We can only hope that our efforts have not fallen too far short of the standards of the distinguished scholar whose work it is.

Gordon M. Kirkwood

Abbreviations Used in the Introduction and Notes

Aesch., *Agam.*: Aeschylus, *Agamemnon*
Aesch., *Suppl.*: Aeschylus, *The Suppliant Maidens*
Aristotle(*Note:* Page and line references given in the margins of the
 translation and in the notes [e.g., 87^{a}38] are to the pagination
 of the complete edition of the works of Aristotle by Imman-
 uel Bekker[Berlin, 1831-36].)
 An. Post.: *Posterior Analytics*
 An. Pr.: *Prior Analytics*
 E. N.: *Nicomachean Ethics*
 Nic. Eth.: *Nicomachean Ethics*
 On Interp.: *On Interpretation*
 Part. An.: *On the Parts of Animals*
 Poet.: *Poetics*
 Pol.: *Politics*
 Rhet.: *Rhetoric*
Athenaeus: Athenaeus, *The Deipnosophistae*
Bywater, Comm.: Ingram Bywater, *Aristotle on the Art of Poetry*,
 Oxford, 1909
CQ: *Classical Quarterly*
Diels, or Diels, *Vorsokratiker*[6]: H. Diels–W. Kranz, *Die Fragmente der
 Vorsokratiker*, 6th ed., 1951
Diogenes Laertius, *Arist.*: Diogenes Laertius, *Lives of the Philosophers*,
 Book 5, Part 1, "Life of Aristotle"
Dionys. Hal.: Dionysius of Halicarnassus
Else: Gerald F. Else, *Aristotle's Poetics: The Argument*, Cambridge,
 Mass., 1957
Eur., *Hipp.*: Euripides, *Hippolytus*
Eustathius, schol. Hom.: Eustathius, *Commentary on Homer's "Iliad"
 and "Odyssey"*
Herrick: Marvin J. Herrick, *The Poetics of Aristotle in England*, New
 Haven, 1930
Hesiod, *Theog.*: Hesiod, *Theogony*
Horace, *A. P.*: Horace, *Ars Poetica*

LSJ: Liddell–Scott–Jones, *Greek-English Lexicon*

Lucas, *Comm.*: D. W. Lucas, *Aristotle's Poetics, Introduction, Commentary, and Appendixes*, Oxford, 1968

Od.: *Odyssey*

Oxyr. Pap.: *The Oxyrhynchus Papyri*, ed. Bernard P. Grenfell and others, London, 1898–1980

Pickard-Cambridge, *Festivals*: A. W. Pickard-Cambridge, *The Dramatic Festivals of Athens*, 2d ed. rev. by John Gould and D. M. Lewis, Oxford, 1968

Pindar, *Ol.*: Pindar, *Olympian Odes*

Plato (*Note:* Page references [e.g., 268D] are to the edition of Plato by H. Stephanus, 1578.)

Rep.: Plato, *Republic*

Quint., *Inst. Orat.*: Quintilian, *Institutes of Oratory*

Rose: V. Rose, ed. of the fragments of Aristotle, Leipzig, 1886

Ross: *The Works of Aristotle*, trans. into English, ed. W. D. Ross. Vol. 12, *Selected Fragments*, Oxford, 1952

Rostagni: see note 78 to the Introduction

Strabo, *Geogr.*: Strabo, *Geography*

ARISTOTLE'S *POETICS*

Introduction

1. *Aristotle*

Aristotle composed the *Poetics* with the Greek tradition of poetry alive before his eyes. To be sure, the epic poem had come to perfection centuries earlier, but the Homeric epics lived as the basis of education and, in professional recitals, were still a form of public entertainment. Tragedy, though its chief development occurred in the fifth century, still made the reputations of brilliant new poets such as Astydamas and Theodectes. The dithyramb,[1] reaching its final, dramatic form, flourished as perhaps never before. Comedy was even then in the process of growth and nearing what Aristotle doubtless would have seen as the fulfillment of its nature in the New Comedy[2] of Philemon and Menander. The pre-eminence of these mimetic forms justifies his treating them as though they alone deserved the name of poetry. So dominant were they that, when in the latter part of the fifth century the Sophists made rhetoric and oratory a self-conscious art, it had seemed only natural to model the style of artistic prose on the language of poetry. Rhetoric, too, was now attaining its full stature in Aristotle's time, which was also the time of Demosthenes and of Isocrates and his school. But among all these voices, another, very different voice had been raised, that of Socrates, bidding the others, in effect, to be silent until men could determine what the words they used really meant, especially words of ethical and social import which poets and rhetoricians uttered so freely. Socrates' art had also developed, broadening into the philosophy of Plato, who in his turn had made, in terms that are difficult to answer, an attempt to rout imitative poetry and rhetoric altogether. Yet in his *Phaedrus* even Plato suggests how rhetoric at least may profit from the new modes of thought. And it is now, in the third generation, that Aristotle enters; without attempting to alter the unalterable nature of poetry and rhetoric, the new discipline of thought can clarify what they are and suggest how they may best attain their ends, which need not be harmful. The clash of science and poetry in the fourth century, when science was new, is paradigmatic for later times.

Aristotle had entered Plato's Academy in 367 B.C. when he was seventeen, the age at which, according to a comic poet of the period,

1

young men made their choice between the horses and philosophers. He was born at Stagira in northern Greece; his father, Nicomachus, who died in Aristotle's boyhood, had been the physician and friend of King Amyntas II of Macedonia, the father of Philip and grandfather of Alexander. Consciousness of belonging to a medical family may have influenced Aristotle's ways of thought; the Macedonian connection certainly played a role in his personal fortunes. The rise and triumph of Macedonian power was the overshadowing historical fact of his time. He remained a member of the Academy for twenty years, until he was thirty-seven, and no doubt in this time advanced his thinking in its characteristic directions; most of his philosophical dialogues were probably published in this period. Perhaps shortly before Plato's death in 347, and perhaps because of an outbreak of anti-Macedonian feeling in Athens, he withdrew to the town of Assos in the Troad, invited thither by Hermeias, the ruler of Assos, and Atarneus, who had himself been a student of the Academy and whose niece and adopted daughter (or perhaps sister) Pythias Aristotle later married. At this time, if not earlier, he came to know Theophrastus, who was thereafter associated with his studies and eventually succeeded him as head of his school. After three years at Assos and two at Mytilene on the neighboring island of Lesbos, he was invited by Philip of Macedon to supervise the education of the thirteen-year-old Alexander; but in 340, when Alexander became regent for his absent father, Aristotle may have retired to Stagira, remaining there until his return to Athens in 335. During these thirteen years of displacement between the ages of thirty-seven and forty-nine, he undoubtedly wrote much, and scholars have found reasons for assigning a number of his works to this period. But we only know for certain that some of the materials for his *History of Animals* came from the vicinity of Lesbos. It is often assumed also that he engaged in teaching and lecturing; for Alexander he is said to have prepared a text of the *Iliad*[3] and to have written treatises *On Monarchy* and (later) *On Colonists*.

Philip was murdered in 336; Alexander speedily completed the conquest of Greece with the destruction of Thebes in September, 335; and the Athenians came to terms with him. Aristotle lost no time in returning to Athens. He did not return to the Academy, however, but formed a school of his own outside the city walls in a grove sacred to Apollo Lycaeus and the Muses, whence the school was later known as the Lyceum, and probably acquired for it the buildings of an existing gymnasium, from whose covered court (*peripatos*) his followers came to be called Peripatetics. The next years were no doubt occupied with teaching and research. His surviving works give us a good idea of the broad range of his lectures. The collection of the constitutions of 158 cities, perhaps begun earlier, was probably now completed. With his relative the historian Callisthenes, he extracted from the archives of Delphi a list of the victors in the Pythian games, and he compiled similar lists of the victors at Olympia, and from the Athenian archives extracted the records of the dramatic contests. He is also said to have collected the first great library of antiquity. In 323, however, the news of Alexander's death in Babylon set off a new wave of anti-Macedonian fervor in Athens. A baseless charge of impiety was brought against Aristotle, and he withdrew to his property at Chalcis in Euboea, a Macedonian stronghold, reportedly saying that the Athenians must not be permitted "to sin twice against philosophy."[4] Here in the next year he died from a chronic ailment at the age of sixty-two.

2. *Aristotle's Involvement with Literature*

In the course of his life, Aristotle may have published some twenty or more books intended for the general public. The greater number of these were the early philosophical dialogues, written in a fluent style admired by Cicero for its richness and sweetness. All these "exoteric" works are lost except for quotations in other ancient writers and perhaps the anonymous *Constitution of Athens*, found in an Egyptian papyrus in 1890. The works we have (about thirty genuine works) are a portion of a large body of writings, not published by Aristotle but apparently kept in his school as the basis of his lectures and accessible to his students. These works are written in a remarkably economical and efficient style, though one by no means devoid of personality, at its best a model for scientific prose but often degenerating into baffling obscurity. All these "esoteric" works, according to a well-known story,[5] were bequeathed by Theophrastus[6] (d. ca. 285 B.C.) to Neleus of Scepsis in the Troad. Later, Neleus' heirs, fearing that the books would be seized by the kings of Pergamum, hid them in a pit, where they suffered from damp and vermin. Eventually, they were purchased and returned to Athens by the bibliophile Apellicon, upon whose death in 84 B.C. they were carried off to Rome by the conqueror Sulla. Here, in the second half of the first century B.C., they were finally edited by Andronicus of Rhodes. It is generally agreed that Andronicus' edition first made the treatises satisfactorily available and that it is the source of our body of Aristotle's works. The success of this edition, which did not include the "exoteric" works, no doubt contributed to the neglect and eventual disappearance of the latter.

From the ancient lists of Aristotle's works, it is apparent that poetry and rhetoric were among his principal interests, though of his writings on these subjects only the *Poetics* and the *Rhetoric* survive. Probably the earliest of all his works was the dialogue *Gryllus* or *On Rhetoric* published in his early twenties. Besides the *Rhetoric* in three books, which we have, several other works on rhetoric are listed, the most important perhaps being a collection or compendium of rhetorical treatises, *Technon Syllogê*, and a compendium of the rhetorical *Art* of Theodectes. A treatise *On Style* in two books is probably identical with the third book of our *Rhetoric*. On the subject of poetry, the dialogue *On Poets* was probably an early work; we return to it below. Our *Poetics* is generally thought to be the first book of a work designated in the lists as *Pragmateia Technês Poêtikês* (*Treatise on the Art of Poetry*) in two books, the second book, presumably containing an account of comedy, being lost to us. A work entitled *Poetica* (*Poetics*) in one book may have been a collection of miscellaneous notes similar to those in Chapters 15–18 of our treatise.[7] The most extensive of Aristotle's works on poetry was the *Homeric Problems* in six books, which bore some close relation to Chapter 25 of our *Poetics*. The *Didascaliae* or records of the dramatic contests at Athens comprised a single book. It is likely that nearly all we know about the dramatic records stems from this work of Aristotle, which is thought to have been the source of the record inscribed on stone and set up in the theater of Dionysus, considerable fragments of which remain. The note on the records of comedy inserted in Chapter 5 of the *Poetics* may reflect these investigations. Related to the *Didascaliae* was the *Dionysiac Victories*, also in one book, conjectured to have been a chronological list of the victors in the dramatic contests, with an indication of the number of their successes. Close to the *Didascaliae* and *Victories*, the catalogues mention a single book *On Tragedies*, which may have contained documentary material not included in those works.[8] Aristotle's own poetry seems to have been of a personal character. We have his affecting "Hymn to Hermeias" so-called and some elegiac verses, including what probably is a eulogy of Plato.

3. *The Dialogue* On Poets

Among the "exoteric" writings, the dialogue *On Poets* would, if we possessed it, undoubtedly throw much light on the *Poetics*. In any case, it was clearly a far more extensive work and earlier. Aristotle himself refers to it (we assume that it is the "published" work intended) at the end of Chapter 15 for the full treatment of the kind of material matters that are not essential to poetry as such but on which poets can often go wrong. Here, at least, he thought of it as supplementing the *Poetics*. And one or two of the quotations we have from it are tantalizingly close to points made in the *Poetics* itself. Thus, in the first book, there was some discussion of the literary dialogue in which the prose mimes of Sophron[9] were treated as "imitations" and Alexamenus of Teos was mentioned as the first to write Socratic dialogues (Ross, frg. 3), the same topic that is touched on very briefly in Chapter 1 of the *Poetics*. Probably, therefore, also to the first book belongs a citation in which Empedocles is called "Homeric" and is praised for his poetical style (frg. 1), since the question of whether Empedocles is a poet is raised in the first chapter of the *Poetics*. In the dialogue, the praise of Empedocles may have been placed in the mouth of a speaker other than Aristotle himself. It is possible, therefore, that the first book of *De Poetis* dealt with poetry as imitation, and conceivable that the dialectical process of division with which imitation is treated in Chapter 1 of the *Poetics* has been adapted from the dialogue. Our only citation from the second book (frg. 6) states that Aristotle criticized Euripides for saying in his *Meleager* that the Aetolians went into battle with the left foot bare, whereas it was the right foot. This has been taken to be one of those "concomitants" of poetry concerning which Aristotle says poets may err. If that is right and if we were then to follow Gerald Else[10] in regarding Chapter 17 of the *Poetics* as continuing this topic, we could assign to the second book of *On Poets* the poet's need to visualize his scenes and feel the passions he portrays and also the description of poets as either men of genius or mad. This last topic would perhaps better suit a dialogue *On Poets* than the *Poetics*. From the third book two items are cited (frgs. 7 and 8), a list of the critics who had assailed various poets and philosophers and a fabulous account of the birth and death of Homer. Little can be made of these, though, to be sure, Aristotle is conscious that many persons had objected to poetry: Xenophanes, Heraclitus,[11] not only Plato, and a myth of sorts might be in place at the end of a dialogue.[12] If from these meager fragments there emerges any shadowy form of the dialogue as a whole, it might be: Book I, "The Nature of Poetry as Imitation"; Book II, "The Procedures Poets Follow"; Book III, "The Poets and Their Critics," which would be roughly similar to the succession of topics in the *Poetics*.

4. The Poetics

The *Poetics* was not published by Aristotle, but has come down to us in the body of "esoteric" works edited by Andronicus.[13] It is written in their efficient style and shows all the anomalies of composition common to these works. These features make it almost certain that it represents a part of Aristotle's program of instruction, and is in fact a major portion of his lectures on poetry, which doubling as a treatise would also probably be available for consultation by his students.[14] Internally, it is structured as an "art" (*technē*) of poetry—that is, it describes what poetry is and lays down what procedures are most effective, viewing poetical composition from within and only marginally from the spectator's point of view. Nevertheless, it is oriented toward an audience desirous of understanding what poetry is, and is not addressed directly to poets. Even "the poets should visualize the scene" or "the poet should make an abstract outline and put in the names later" is said to the audience or reader. As an "art" of poetry, it parallels Aristotle's *Rhetoric*, which is also an "art." Indeed, this parallel may account for the origin of the *Poetics*. "Arts" of rhetoric already existed in some numbers (Aristotle made a collection of them), but, though poetry had always been regarded as an art, no one hitherto, as far as we know, had produced an "art" of poetry.[15] The *Poetics* may very well, therefore, owe its existence and its form to the unique circumstances that led Aristotle to include poetics with the art of rhetoric in his program. These circumstances seem already to have existed during Aristotle's membership in the Academy; his first lectures on rhetoric have been traced to this period, and it is probable that they were accompanied from the beginning by the lectures on poetry.[16] These seem to have come in his course immediately before the lectures on rhetoric.[17] We are told that Aristotle lectured on the more abstruse subjects in the mornings and on subjects such as rhetoric in the afternoons.[18] Perhaps we may imagine the *Poetics* as afternoon lectures, delivered by the meticulously attired lecturer with his characteristic lisp.[19]

5. Outline of the Poetics

The basic outline of the *Poetics* is clear and easy to follow. The forms of Imitation are distinguished as to the means, the objects, and the manner of imitation with the aim of producing definitions of epic poetry, tragedy, and comedy (Chapters 1–3); the three forms are sharply marked off (Chapter 5), and the lecturer proceeds first to deal with tragedy, stating its definition and deriving therefrom the fact that tragedy consists of six "parts," only four of which, however (plot, character, thought, and language), are of direct concern to the poet's art (Chapter 6); he discusses these four "parts," expanding especially on plot (Chapters 7–14) and language (Chapters 19–22), and then turns to epic poetry (Chapters 23–24), handling it briefly, without definition, since in most essentials it coincides with tragedy, and ending with a comparison of tragedy and epic in order to show that the common function (the stirring of pity and fear) is best performed by tragedy. He is now ready to deal with comedy, as promised in Chapter 6, but our *Poetics* ends abruptly at this point.

This smooth development is, however, interrupted by several major intrusions: an account of the origin and growth of poetry (Chapter 4); the external parts of tragedy (Chapter 12); a miscellany of empirical observations (from mid-Chapter 15 to the end of Chapter 18), some of them expanded (Chapters 16 and 17) and others (Chapter 18) little more than memoranda; a grammatical study (Chapter 20) having little to do with poetics; and a chapter (26) on literary criticism. Among these sections are some of the most interesting parts of the *Poetics*, and all (unless Chapter 20) are very pertinent to the general method of the treatise; their fault is that they break into a train of thought. At the same time, they are not wildly misplaced; each comes at a point in the argument at which the lecturer (with some oral explanation) could use it. It is only natural that lectures, no doubt repeated over the years, should acquire such accretions, and all the surviving works of Aristotle have similar features. However, some of these digressions, and especially the first two, may have been inserted almost from the beginning; others no doubt are later.[20] There are also passages throughout the *Poetics* in which it is suspected that notes written by Aristotle in the margins of his manuscript have been clumsily introduced into the text.[21] More disturbing, as affecting the main argument, is the discrepancy between Chapters 13 and 14, the first preferring the unhappy ending for the overall "change of fortune" and the second preferring a happy outcome for the main tragic incident. There seems to be no satisfactory explanation of this oversight. It is also disconcerting to find a term carefully defined in one place and elsewhere used in disregard of the definition: *muthos*, defined as "plot," sometimes means "myth" or "story"; *ethos* (character) is defined as "a habit of moral choice" but elsewhere has its usual meaning of "having individual traits" or "character portrayal"; *pathos* is defined as "physical suffering" but more often has its common meaning of "passion" or "emotion."

Poetry, which played so conspicuous a role in Greek life, had inevitably been the subject of much discussion before the time of Plato and Aristotle, though we can be fairly sure that the *Poetics* had no important predecessor as a systematic study of the art.[22] Within the *Poetics*, material drawn from outside sources tends to appear as an excrescence on the argument—for example, the Dorian claims to the invention of drama (Chapter 2), the external parts of tragedy (Chapter 12), Protagoras' observations on language (Chapter 19)—though at times such material is more essential—for example, details relating to the development of tragedy (Chapter 4) and Glaucon's comments on critics (Chapter 25). Indeed, the whole of Chapter 25 is necessarily close to the traditional discussions of Homer. Where Aristotle argues against unnamed opponents, as in Chapter 13, against those who preferred the double ending and disparaged Euripides, and, in Chapter 26, against those who preferred epic poetry to tragedy, it is possible that he refers to persons within the Academy or his own school rather than to published works.[23]

It is more important to be aware of the probability that the two fundamental assumptions of the *Poetics*—that poetry is imitation and that pity and fear are the emotions especially involved in tragedy—were current before Plato and Aristotle wrote. Both are treated by Aristotle as axioms that do not require proof. In fact, both ideas are perhaps discernible in what we have from the Sophist Gorgias, the founder of the theory of artistic prose, whose authority was very great at the end of the fifth century.[24] In his *Encomium of Helen*, Gorgias celebrates the sovereign power of Discourse, the *Logos* or Word, whether in prose or verse, as magical in its effects and penetrating the soul for good or ill as a drug or medicine penetrates the body, its aim, however, being to give pleasure rather than to convey truth.

All poetry (he says) I think of and denominate as *logos* with meter. As people listen to it there comes upon them a great shuddering of fear and tearful pity and a strong desire for lamentation; through its words, the soul experiences an emotion of its own for the good or bad fortune that comes to the business and bodies of others.

It is likely that Gorgias thinks chiefly here of epic and tragic poetry, and the words he uses for pity and fear are those used by Aristotle. Evidence that Gorgias thought of poetry as imitation is less clear. Among the powers of the *logos* he included the power to deceive, and he seems to have regarded deception *(apate)*—we may say dramatic illusion—as that which the tragic poet in particular aims to effect.[25] Tragedy gives pleasure through a deception "in which the deceiver is more just than the non-deceiver and the deceived wiser than the non-deceived," meaning that the successful poet "fulfils his obligation to deceive and that it is the sensitive spectator who is transported by the charm of the words."[26] That "deception" involves the idea of imitation is suggested by the words of a contemporary follower of Gorgias:[27] "The best tragic poet and the best painter are those who most deceive by making things resembling the real ones." That is, by imitating them, but the word "imitate" does not occur to him, and in fact "imitation" used distinctly of the poet's function seems not to be found before Plato.[28] Gorgias' word "deception" is prejudicial and probably paradoxical; "imitation" is neutral, but as used for the poet's work in Plato's *Republic*, it generally means deception—impersonation instead of honest narrative, imitation of a shoemaker by a poet who does not know how to make shoes. Indeed, Plato seems to accept the whole of Gorgias' description of rhetoric and poetry, if only as a basis for denouncing them—that they aim only at pleasure; that tragedy stirs up a desire for lamentation; that their imitations ignorantly or willfully deceive.[29] Aristotle, though writing from a point of view favorable to the poet, no doubt owes the concept of imitation together with the term itself directly to Plato, generally employing it in the broad sense of *Republic* 10, 603C, "the imitation of men in action." Terms like *apate*, when translated as "deception" or "dramatic illusions," lead to nothing; "imitation," on the other hand, opens up the possibility of the whole *Poetics* of Aristotle. The abrupt announcement at the beginning of the *Poetics* that certain kinds of poems are "imitations" perhaps presupposes a discussion of this subject in the first book of the dialogue *On Poets*.

Whatever may have been the background of these ideas, the argument based on them, the substance of the *Poetics*, could have been conceived nowhere outside the school of Plato. Socrates, Plato, and Aristotle himself had in effect discovered the methods of controlled and self-conscious thought that lead to a grasp of the essentials of any subject. The hallmark of these methods is the definition, and the *Poetics*—at least the first half of it—may almost be described as a tissue of definitions, both definitions of "substance" (e.g., the definition of tragedy) and "dictionary" definitions (e.g., "by plot I mean ... ").[30]

6. *The Method of the* Poetics

The *Poetics* becomes more luminous for us if we follow Aristotle in his conscious application of method and grasp what therefore is going on in the treatise. It must always be kept in mind that the *Poetics* is not about poetry in some vague sense of the word but about the art of poetry; it is an "art" or *technê* (how to compose successful poems), but an "art" that is founded on a scientific understanding of the subject. Aristotle divides the sciences into the theoretical, the practical, and the productive. As sciences, all have knowledge as their purpose, the theoretical sciences (e.g., mathematics) knowledge for its own sake, the practical sciences (e.g., ethics) knowledge for the sake of conduct, the productive sciences (e.g., poetics) knowledge for the sake of making something.[31] Perhaps nowhere else in Aristotle's works is scientific method, as described by him in his *Analytics*, so open and unconcealed as in this short treatise.

Aristotle's advice to anyone who may be composing a handbook (*pragmateia*) on a subject that is a generic whole is that he should first divide the genus into its primary species and then examine the properties peculiar to the species, working through the nearest common *differentiae*. That is, he should find the definition of each species and deduce from the definition the essential properties of the species. These will necessarily be the properties of the genus, since the genus has no existence apart from its species.[32] This is the procedure followed by Aristotle himself in his *pragmateia* of the art of poetry, allowance being made for the nature of the subject. Poetry as imitation is divided into its species, and from the definition of one of these, tragedy, it is deduced that this particular species or form has six essential properties or parts.[33] Thus, the important steps are (1) the establishment of the definitions of the species and (2) the deduction of their properties. For the establishment of definitions Aristotle goes on to recommend the method of *diaeresis* or division through *differentiae* or differences— that is, in the definition of a species the genus is named and the differences that mark this species off from all others are enumerated. Tragedy is an imitation in language and in dramatic form of the actions of serious persons. No other species of imitation has all these differences. This method of defining species, which we take for granted, was then relatively new, having been discovered by Plato apparently in mid-career and employed by him and by the members of the Academy in various ways. The definition, however, though useful, only gathers up what we already know; it is a formula from which the essential properties may be inferred. The process of inference is basically Aristotle's own great discovery, the syllogism. The finding of the "parts" or essential properties is the scientific goal, and in fact the durability of the *Poetics* largely rests on the discovery of the six parts and the discussion of them, particularly the discussion of plot.

In another place,[34] Aristotle puts the matter succinctly: "A single science is the science of a single genus, comprising all the things (i. e. species) compounded out of the primary elements (i. e. out of the genus and *differentiae*) and all the parts or essential properties of these species."[35] The opening statement of the *Poetics* virtually repeats this formulation. The treatise will discuss the art of poetry as a genus and hence its various species and their parts.[36] Let us begin, Aristotle says, with the primary elements, and accordingly what follows in Chapters 1 through 3 is concerned only with the genus (imitation) and its *differentiae*.[37] The *differentiae* are usefully classified (following Plato) under means, objects, and manner of imitation; but *differentiae* and genus are not formally combined into definitions of species until a definition is needed in Chapter 6. What intervenes at this point, in Chapter 4, is of exceptional interest.

Chapter 4 on the origin and development of the art of poetry aims, somewhat like a Platonic myth, to show the terms of the abstract *diaeresis* as existing in reality. As a genus, imitation is only a potential-ity and exists nowhere except as actualized in its species, or rather in individual acts or works of imitation. Chapter 4 shows it as actualized as poetry in general, as serious or ludicrous poetry, and finally and most perfectly in tragedy and comedy. The keynote of the chapter is "na-ture," and we pass from potential nature—the natural impulse to imi-tate and to delight in imitations—to the perfected "nature" of tragedy.[38] A few historical facts are adduced as lending certainty to the argument. The role of the poets, improvising and, in the case of trag-edy, only gradually comprehending the requirements of the form, an-ticipates their role in later passages of the treatise. They imitate instinctively, not primarily for the sake of giving pleasure to others, but others just as instinctively take pleasure in the imitations, and both instincts are essential to the creation of the art. The proposition that all men delight in imitations is impressively demonstrated in a formal proof through "signs" and "causes."[39] Pleasure (which need not be mindless) is the only external purpose for poetry that the *Poetics* rec-ognizes.

As the basic argument resumes, comedy, tragedy, and epic poetry are briefly distinguished from one another (Chapter 5), and Aristotle turns first (Chapter 6) to the definition of the essence *(ousia)* of tragedy, "gathering it up"[40] from what has already been said:

> Tragedy is an imitation of an action that is serious, complete, and possessing magnitude; in embellished language, each kind of which is used separately in the different parts; in the mode of action and not narrated; and effecting through pity and fear [what we call] the "catharsis" of such emotions.

That the appropriate *differentiae* from the *diaeresis* have all been col-lected is clear once Aristotle has explained that "embellished lan-guage" carries with it rhythm and melody. We note, however, that it is not the persons, but the action that is now described as "serious" and is the "object" of imitation, a point perhaps intended in Chapter 2 but not made clear. There are important elements in the definition that are not derived from the *diaeresis* at all, as we shall observe presently. Aristotle's only concern immediately following the definition is to complete the scientific process by determining the essential "parts" or attributes of the species. A definition is only a formula summarizing the appropriate *differentiae*, and it is from the *differentiae* that the parts are now deduced in a formal demonstration (*since* in dramatic forms, *therefore necessarily* spectacle is a part, etc.). Aristotle is at pains to show that the six parts—plot, character, thought, language, spectacle, and music—allow for all three modalities—means, object, and manner—and that they are certainly essential attributes since they are "true in every instance."[41] By assigning "serious" to the action rather than to the agents, and, in the demonstration which immediately follows the definition, by describing the agents indefinitely as "having a certain quality of character and thought," he has generalized the "parts" so that they apply to a genus (drama) that includes tragedy; tragedy cannot exist without them, but they may be found together apart from tragedy—viz., in comedy.[42] An advantage of generalization here is that the parts can be presented in the rest of Chapter 6 simply for themselves as "forms the poets use" without the complication of specific tragic qualities. These will be taken up beginning with Chapter 7. The attributes are called parts because added together they complete the notion of the dramatic form, and we may perhaps infer that the parallel organization of animal species out of "parts" is here not far from Aristotle's mind.[43]

We need not suppose that the six parts were *discovered* by deduction; presumably they were found by simple observation and induction. In fact, the words "and beyond these there are no others" probably express the defiance of one who believes he has made a complete induction. The point is that, however arrived at, the parts can be proved by demonstration to be essential—that is, to have a necessary relationship to the definition. Even so, we need not expect a demonstration in poetics to be as stringent as a demonstration in mathematics.

The constituent parts are not all of equal importance; in fact, plot, though a "part," is the final cause *(telos)* of the other parts and analogous to the soul or life principle in animals.[44] Aristotle lists the parts in order of importance—after plot, character is second, thought third, and language fourth. This order presumably depends on the degree to which the several parts function to serve the plot. It is worth reminding ourselves at this point that Aristotle is not merely theorizing; the relative importance of the parts reflects actual experience. In Aristotle's experience, tragic plots were almost without exception the imitations of known myths whose main lines could not be altered; this, in turn, limited the characterization of the agents—e.g., of a Clytemnestra or an Orestes—and, to a lesser degree, limited what they could find to say to each other (thought), while language, as abstracted from thought and character, was least governed by plot and most governed by the discretion of the poet.

Since the *Poetics* is concerned only with the poet's art, music and spectacle, useful as *differentiae* in the *diaeresis*, are virtually laid aside, and plot, character, thought, and language supply the framework for the substantial discussion of tragedy that follows.

We may surmise that the *diaeresis* of Chapters 1 through 3, which has successfully provided a rational background for the "parts," was set up chiefly for that very purpose. To supply all the *differentiae* that would yield a stringent definition of tragedy, though theoretically possible, would be tedious and impractical. A definition only calls to our attention what we already know. Accordingly, Aristotle has not scrupled to add to the definition the properties or qualities that are requisite for tragedy. The proprium or peculiarity *(idion)* of this form, he says later (1452ᵇ33), is that it is "the imitation of things fearful and pitiful."⁴⁵ This appears in the definition as the special capacity of tragedy to effect a "purgation" through such an imitation. He has also placed in the definition the requirement that the action imitated be not only serious, but also complete and possessing magnitude. These indispensable qualities of the action—the pitiful and fearful, completeness, and magnitude—certainly have not been "gathered up" from the *diaeresis*, and "gathered up" can only refer to the *differentiae* that will yield the six parts. These six parts he wishes to see at first uncolored by qualities; but they only become parts of tragedy when the action imitated is so qualified. Hence, the parts provide the framework for the ensuing discussion of tragedy, and the qualities provide the substance of what is said of plot, which is the imitation of the action.

Completeness is studied in Chapters 7 through 12, magnitude in Chapter 7, pity and fear in Chapters 13 and 14, and embellished language in Chapters 21 and 22.

If a poem is to have the maximum pleasurable effect, the action selected for imitation must be a whole and complete so that the plot that imitates the action may have these same qualities. The idea of organic unity had been set forth in Plato's *Phaedrus* (264C): "Every discourse *(logos)* ought to be constructed like an animal, having a body of its own, so as not to be without a head or feet, but to have a middle and extremities suited to one another and to the whole." This is likely to be the origin of Aristotle's famous description of beginning, middle, and end in Chapter 7, where the animal comparison becomes explicit immediately afterward in the allied discussion of magnitude.⁴⁶ For a tragedy, which is the imitation of an action, organic unity of beginning, middle, and end simply means that from beginning to end the events of the plot should proceed in a necessary or probable sequence. The phrase, repeated so often, represents Aristotle's analysis of events *(pragmata)* as formulated, for example, in his *Topics* (112ᵇ1): "Some things occur of necessity, others usually [hence probably], by chance." Clearly, only events that proceed by necessity or probability will produce a unity, as a series of chance events will not, even if they happen to one man (Chapter 8). A sequence of events is "necessary" when experience tells us that the one event is such as *always* follows from the other, and is "probable" when we know that the one event *usually* follows from the other. For most of the ethical situations of tragedy, probability is no doubt enough.[47] "What men know to happen or not to happen, to be or not to be, for the most part thus and thus, is a probability, e.g., 'the envious hate,' 'the beloved shows affection.' "[48] It seems probable that Oedipus, being proud and quick-tempered, should slay an offensive stranger. The particular act falls within the universal expectation of what an irascible man may do under provocation. In real life, an Oedipus may not act thus "in character" on every occasion, but in poetry (particularly in a Greek tragedy of 1600 lines) he must do so. Poetry has to convince us that the events it describes are possible, and it does so by confining itself to such events as are probable or necessary.[49] In order to be intelligible and win assent, poetry is thus forced to aim at universality, since the necessary and the probable are universals.[50] History is under no such constraint; it does not usually have to convince us that the events it describes are possible—what has happened must have been possible—and this makes all the difference; history is not obliged by its very nature, as poetry is, to relate only probable or necessary sequences. Many of the events of history come about by chance or fortune. Poetry, therefore, is inevitably drawn toward the universal and consequently is more philosophical than history, since philosophy also is constrained to deal only with universals.

Thus, completeness implies probability, and probability implies universality. The quality an individual poet may give to his universal situations is not the concern of the general theory. No doubt if he gives us fresh insights into human nature, so much the better (a cultured audience is not likely to take pleasure in stock responses); but the poetical universals exist not for the purpose of enlightening the spectator or teaching him something he did not know, but solely for the purpose of giving pleasure by making the imitation recognizable and convincing to a normal mind. Though poetry is thus bound to be in some degree philosophical, the poets themselves need not be philosophers. The power of universalizing or generalizing is the common possession of the human mind as such. How this comes to be is described by Aristotle in the fascinating last chapter of his *Posterior Analytics*. What we call experience (based on sense perception and memory) is the possession of universals, and in this, he says, originates "the skill of the craftsman and the knowledge of the man of science, skill in the sphere of coming to be and science in the sphere of being."

Magnitude is studied along with completeness in Chapter 7. The topic is important as bearing on the beauty and the dignity of the tragic poem. In Chapter 4, we have seen the poet-craftsmen forming by experience more and more adequate notions (universals) of the form of tragedy, including a notion of magnitude as tragedy grew out of its initial small plots and ridiculous language into a sizable and solemn form attractive to serious poets. In Chapter 5, it appears that the end of this empirical process was to settle for an action occupying roughly one revolution of the sun, though at earlier stages the indefinite time span of epic had been tried in tragedy as well. Now, in Chapter 7, the man of science views the question within the sphere of "being"—i.e., with a detached understanding of the nature of the case. He frees tragedy from the external exigencies of stage presentation and asserts that the longer the play is, while remaining perspicuous, the finer it will be, since beauty inheres in largeness, and in general that the appropriate length will be achieved if the change of fortune required in tragedy is developed through a close succession of probable events. These are intelligible principles on which the quality of a tragedy can be judged, and obviously superior to a rule of thumb like "one revolution of the sun."

The one distinguishing mark of tragedy is that it imitates piteous and fearful things; whether it ends happily or unhappily is not essential (1452^{a}39-^{b}3, 33). Chapter 13 deals with pity and fear in the overall structure of a play, the "change of fortune," Chapter 14 with pity and fear in the individual tragic deed. In both cases, the poet ought to know what arrangements he should choose and what he should avoid, and hence Aristotle uses the same method throughout: he mentions all the possible arrangements and points out the best. That all the possible arrangements are found is assured by dichotomy—good or not good (bad) men coming to a good or bad end; the violent deed done either by friend or nonfriend (enemy or indifferent); the deed either done or not done, and if done, done wittingly or not wittingly. In the first case, however, that of good or bad men coming to good or bad ends, none of the alternatives proves acceptable for a tragic effect; but ethical goodness and badness admit a third possibility, the man between, neither eminently good and just (hence his downfall does not shock us) nor yet falling into misfortune through depravity, but rather through a mistake or error (*hamartia*) on his part. Here Aristotle has neatly applied his general theory of logical contraries (*Categories* 10, 11^{b}33 ff.). Some contraries, he notes, such as black and white or good and bad, admit intermediates and some intermediates have names, such as gray and other shades between black and white, while others have no names and have to be defined as *not* either extreme, "as in the case of that which is neither good nor bad, neither just nor unjust." A bad man may err, but an eminently just (hence intelligent) man probably will not err; the intermediate man may probably err and yet not be bad. In fact, Aristotle here shades his character toward the good. In the second case, that of the best choice among tragic deeds, the possibilities have only to be listed and a choice made among them. That Aristotle's preference is for the happy peripety, which will make an unhappy ending improbable, clearly does not square with his preference for the unhappy ending in Chapter 13.[51]

Once the consideration of plot is ended, the intellectual energy of the *Poetics* noticeably slackens. Of the remaining "parts," two, Character and Thought, get brief treatment, and between them (from the middle of Chapter 15 to the end of Chapter 18) there falls a section of practical and empirical observations, set down in no particular order, which because of its empirical nature has been judged to be a late addition made when Aristotle was no longer in the grip of Platonic theory.[52] The last "part," Language, is treated at greater length in Chapters 21 and 22.[53] First, the kinds of words are enumerated—current or common words, foreign words, metaphors, etc.—and then the "virtue" of style is found in a mixture of common and uncommon, the common giving clarity, the uncommon distinction. Aristotle shows how the two can be extremes, and the "virtue" of style evidently is established by the principle of the "mean" familiar to us from his ethical works. The mixture or mean will be different for different types of poetry. For the spoken parts of tragedy—the lyric parts are not within the province of Aristotle's poet—the mixture will not be different from that of prose or good conversation. Other types of poetry—e.g., dithyramb and epic—will tolerate a stronger admixture of uncommon words. We hear nothing of the language of pity and fear, nor should we expect to do so at this point; we have heard of this in Chapter 19, under Thought. The chapters on style are a final abstraction and a useful one; but the dynamic functions of language, as we tend to think of language, fall for Aristotle under Thought as *logoi*, speeches, rather than under *lexis* or speech[54]—speeches "proving and refuting, stirring up emotions (pity, fear, anger, etc.), and enlarging or belittling the importance of things." The cross reference in Chapter 19 to the *Rhetoric* (especially to Book 2) is not idle. Aristotle's division between Thought, what is said, and Style, the poet's overall way of saying it, has been a pitfall for some modern students of the *Poetics;* the division is the critic's—the poet, of course, spontaneously expresses the desired thought in whatever his style may be. And style, thus abstracted, is properly regarded as a "part" of tragedy, since it has a place in the effect. One can compose a tragedy in the highly wrought style of Aeschylus, but Aristotle evidently thinks that the style of Euripides, closer to living speech, better serves the purposes of tragic mimesis.[55]

With Language Aristotle concludes his discussion of tragedy and its parts, and he now turns to epic poetry; but since the essential identity of these two forms has been shown in Chapter 5, and almost all that has been said of tragedy applies, therefore, to epic as well, it is only necessary here to insist that an epic poem should have dramatic unity (Chapter 23) and to point out those features in which it differs from tragedy (Chapter 24). Before proceeding to a final comparison of tragedy and epic poetry, Aristotle has introduced his admirable chapter (25) on literary criticism, giving weight and a lift in interest to a lecture that is running out. In method it is perhaps the most orderly and sustained section of the *Poetics:* sound critical principles are laid down and applied to a dozen examples divided between criticisms involving the basic art (imitation) and those involving the medium (language), to reach the conclusion that these criticisms can be reduced to five classes.[56] However, the chapter is oriented toward the outside world of traditional criticism, not inward to the *Poetics*—we hear nothing here of inconsistent character drawing or the mishandling of denouement; in fact, the term "imitation" is here used in the sense of representation and does not reflect the wider use of the word in the main argument of the *Poetics.*[57] The method of the last chapter (26) may be called rhetorical; Aristotle parries the charge that tragedy is vulgar by turning it off onto the actors, and having thus put tragedy on a level with epic, he offers proofs to show that it is actually superior in fulfilling the artistic aim. This is the procedure of the rhetorical *encomium* (cf. *Rhetoric* 1.9), and we note that while the vices of epic are stressed, its virtues as touched on in Chapter 24 are suppressed; but it seems probable and we are convinced. Plato, who preferred epic recitation (*Laws* 396), perhaps would not have been convinced.

From Chapter 4, we gather that the major divisions of poetry are tragedy and comedy, and in Chapter 6 Aristotle promises to discuss comedy after epic poetry. Comedy is distinguished from tragedy/epic in Chapter 5 and commended for its universality in Chapter 9, but mostly it is carefully kept out of the *Poetics* as we have it, not even coming under consideration in the very general treatment of language and literary criticism. Clearly, Aristotle is reserving comedy for special, and probably extended, treatment, and if the *Poetics* represents lectures given repeatedly over many years, it seems inconceivable that he left his promise to treat it unfulfilled. We can only guess about the methods he may have employed, but it seems probable that he would have made something of the six parts of drama, would have emphasized comic character, and hence ludicrous actions (Chapter 5), and would have seen comedy as approaching its norm or *phusis* in his own day with generalized humor, not personal invective, and with "proba-ble" plots (Chapter 9); he is also prepared (Chapter 22) with a formula for comic language.

What we have seen is that Aristotle isolates problems and applies in each case a method that seems appropriate to clarify it, always very consciously. It remains to notice the most important aspect of method of all—at least the most important for the reader of the *Poetics* to have in mind. This is the restrictive or departmentalizing character of the treatise, which is unswervingly maintained throughout. It does not study poetry in its social or moral implications; it is essential to keep in mind that it is not a treatise on poetry, but an *art* of poetry. It is not a defense of poetry; it aims only to discover for each kind of poetry the form that will best realize its capacity—in the case of tragedy, the form that will best give pleasure through the imitation of pitiful and fearful events. And in this case also it is further restricted to the poet's own art, leaving aside those "parts," Spectacle and Music, that are not completely within the poet's control. The "parts" Character (Chapter 15) and Thought (Chapter 19) are handled very briefly; a few general points are made as relating to tragedy, and Aristotle stops short; to treat these large subjects more broadly would involve more than the art of poetry. For Thought, Aristotle refers to his *Rhetoric*; for Character a reference to his *Ethics* would perhaps be less pertinent.[58] In serious poetry, the characters are required to be "good," not for the sake of affording models of conduct, but because the fortunes and misfortunes of vicious characters would not elicit from the normal spectator or reader the response proper to this kind of poetry. Everything is viewed from within the poet's art; in the chapter on literary criticism (25), irrationalities, unseemly stories about the gods, what may seem to be immoral actions, and mistakes in regard to some other art are seen to be justifiable if they further the poet's artistic aim. All procedures are stripped down to bare functions of the art; the quality an individual poet may give to them cannot be prescribed. When Homer is praised, it is always for a definite technical reason. Mistakes about the *Poetics* have been made by those who have not understood its restrictive method. No doubt Aristotle could have discussed the moral and social value of poetry, and perhaps would have done so in an unfinished part of his *Politics*, where this would have been within his method; there is no reason to suppose that he did not personally respond to the lofty thought or exquisite language of an Aeschylus or a Sophocles. And on the other hand, it is probably unsafe to ascribe anything in the *Poetics* to mere personal bias or preference.

Aristotle's mode of thinking on any subject is commonly described as teleological. He tends to regard the processes of nature and the activities of human beings alike as purposive, as pursued for some end *(telos)*. As for the purpose of poetry, he simply accepts the common view from Homer to Plato that poetry exists to give pleasure to the audience or reader. Poetry is essentially imitation; we imitate instinctively and instinctively take pleasure in imitations. *The pleasure of poetry comes primarily from the fact of imitation.* Pleasure in rhythm or elevated language is secondary and not peculiar to poetry. The different forms of poetry have each a special capacity *(dynamis)*, realizable in its effect *(ergon)*, and function dictates form. Hence, epic poetry, which aims at the same effect as tragedy, has historically been replaced by tragedy, a form that realizes the common aim more effectively. We take pleasure even in the imitation of unpleasant things. The imitation of grief and terror in tragedy gives us the special pleasure of tragedy, which Aristotle calls "purgation" *(catharsis)*; we feel relief from the bitter imitation. Tragedy is ranged with the "cathartic" arts as giving pleasure through the representation, not of agreeable, but of disturbing emotions.[59]

Though the effect on the normal cultivated spectator is the limiting criterion of the form, the *Poetics* is not directly concerned with the spectator's reactions. Its concern is with the internal structure of the tragic form, and its teleology is usually "internal," as in the case of an animal species.[60] But this is not worked out quite as we might expect it to be. Assuredly, the plot as the life and soul of tragedy is the *telos*, which the other "parts" serve much as the body in man and animals is said to serve the soul; but Aristotle, as we have seen, does not show much interest in describing how the "parts" render this service. No doubt he avoids what would be a confusing infinity of varying relationships; he knows of tragedies that are altogether lacking in character portrayal (1150[a]25) and other "ethical" tragedies (1456[a]1) in which presumably character was the salient feature.[61] This is a wide sweep. Instead, his interest in structure more practically centers in the organization of the plot itself as a synthesis of events having beginning, middle, and end and parts of its own in recognitions, reversals, and fatal deeds. It is in this organization of plot rather than in the more distant organization of the species that he, like Plato, sees an analogy with organic life. Epic poetry, like tragedy, should embody a single unified action "so that like a whole unified animal it may produce its proper pleasure" (1459[a]20).

From what has been said, it is evident that the *Poetics* is not set up as an answer to Plato's moral and metaphysical objections to poetry nor to meet Plato's challenge to the lovers of poetry to come forward and prove that it is profitable to the state and to human life (*Republic* 10, 607D). Plato judges poetry in its moral and social effects; the *Poet-*

ics studies poetry strictly in its own nature. Objectively, the *Poetics* presents an idea of poetry that does not differ from Plato's: it is an imitation of human life; it aims at emotional pleasure, not moral instruction; it takes one of three forms—narrative, dramatic, or mixed; it represents gods doing wrong acts; it tolerates incorrectness in representing the special arts; its products should be artistic wholes.[62] For Plato, poetical imitation is a deception, since the poet must imitate a great number of persons and things without having real knowledge of any of them; and pure dramatic form is morally inferior to narrative since it is more deceptive and appeals especially to a vulgar audience, while to stir up the emotions without any moral aim is to feed the unruly part of our nature at the expense of the ruling mind. The *Poetics* offers some corrections, by the way: tragedy at least is not more vulgar than epic if you consider the poem and not the theatrical performance. Whereas Plato asserts that poets (*Republic* 364) represent bad men as triumphing, Aristotle points out that this is not tragic at all. Though in the name of *catharsis* emotion will be aroused and susceptible spectators will weep as unrestrainedly in Aristotle's audience as in that of Gorgias or Plato, this concept suggests with its emphasis on relief that for most persons the effect of tragedy is a "harmless pleasure."[63] This is to differ from Plato, not to answer him. And in general the *Poetics* ignores the doubts raised by an idealistic philosophy. For Plato, the poetry that mirrors the actions of men, their joys and their sorrows, is twice removed from the truth; anyone who has glimpsed the truth and anyone who has been trained from infancy to respond rightly to pleasure and pain must feel contempt for an art that elicits tears for tragic errors. The *Poetics* does not deny that this may be so. Poetry is said to be more philosophical and higher in the scale than History (which doubtless mirrors the actions of men) because it tends to represent ethical universals based on probability. This no doubt gives to poetry a dignity that Plato denies for it; but probability is not a principle with which Plato would rest content.

Plato, like Gorgias, tends to think of rhetoric and poetry as kindred arts. His charge against both is that they use the great power of discourse harmfully, in ignorance or disregard of truth and goodness. The rhetorical speaker convinces his audience that what he says is true and what he advocates is good, without himself knowing what truth and goodness are; the poet deceives the spectators with necessarily false images of life, aiming only to please and not to better them; and both arts play recklessly upon the emotions. Tragedy is a kind of rhetoric that flatters the multitude (*Gorgias* 502A). The indictment is brought in discourses in dialogue form, combining at once the essence of rhetoric, persuasion, and the essence of poetry, imitation, and written in a seductive style somewhere between poetry and prose that betrays the influence of Gorgias. But the persuasion of the dialogue takes the form of a rigorous sifting of thought aimed at discovering what is really true and good, and the imitation of men engaged in this activity is an imitation of something that Plato really knows, while the pleasure it gives, enhanced by charm of style, looks beyond to the intellectual and moral betterment of the reader. This union of rhetoric and poetry, animated by the spirit of truth, would seem to be the Gorgianic *Logos* raised to the highest power, against which as a norm common rhetoric and common poetry may be measured. With regard to truth, both sophistic rhetoric and poetry are imitations and both are persuasive, but rhetoric is intentionally persuasive, poetry inadvertently and insidiously.[64] There is hope, therefore, for rhetoric (which is only straightforward discourse enhanced and methodized), if it learns from philosophy to serve the cause of truth and justice (*Phaedrus* 277B7–278D7); but there is no hope for imitative poetry, which is flawed at the root by a vicious use of imitation and is without moral purpose. In his *Statesman* (304 A–D), Plato recognizes a kind of rhetoric or oratory that partakes of the "kingly art" and guides the affairs of state by persuading men to observe justice, whereas poetry (here called mythography) is a kind of rhetoric that "persuades the multitude but does not teach."

To the recognized connection between rhetoric and poetry the *Poetics* may be said to owe its origin and more than one decisive feature of its doctrine. The connection would make it natural for Aristotle to include poetics with rhetoric in his program, and, as we have seen, the result would be to produce an "art" of poetry, probably the first of its kind, on the model of the already traditional "arts" of rhetoric. These "arts" themselves, to be sure, may well have touched on poetry as well as prose. The theory of the emotions seems to have been developed for the sake of rhetoric, where it has broader scope than we find in the *Poetics*, and it may be that rhetorical theory is the background from which Gorgias or another distinguished pity and fear as the emotions primarily evoked by tragedy.[65] One can speak more definitely about the principle of Probability, which belongs primarily to rhetorical theory, where it had figured prominently from the beginning in the fifth century. Aristotle would readily see that probability is equally applicable to the rhetoric that convinces but does not teach, and he has made of it the cornerstone of the *Poetics*. The insistence with which he presses this principle throughout perhaps hints that its importance for poetry is his personal discovery. At all events, we may think, it is this principle that makes rhetoric and poetics subjects worthy of the attention of a philosophical school. Rhetoric proper, relying at its best on the probable syllogism or enthymeme, is the "counterpart" of dialectic (*Rhet.* 1.1); poetry, in describing events that are probable and might happen, turns upon universals and is more philosophical than history.[66] Probability is the philosophy of real life, the level on which oratory and drama have their existence.

For both Plato and Aristotle, however, poetry is an autonomous art, distinguished from rhetoric by its form of imitation and by the fact that its sole aim is to give pleasure. One art, to be sure, may serve as material for another, "architectonic" art, as horsemanship may serve the military art (*Nicomachean Ethics* 1.1). When in this way rhetoric serves poetry, supplying a whole "part" of tragedy—i.e., Thought (Chapter 19)—and thereby in fact most of the verbal tissue of the play, the result is poetry, not rhetoric, even when the personages talk like rhetoricians. If an imitative artist were to shape his imitation with the aim of bringing home to the spectator some general idea or teaching a practical lesson, thus making his work a mere *exemplum* calculated to enforce his thesis through poetical pleasure, the result would be not poetry but rhetoric and propaganda. If the poetical imitation is subordinated to the art of dialectic, as in Plato's dialogues, the result no doubt is philosophy and not poetry.

In Plato's *Apology*, Socrates asks the poets what their poems mean. They are unable to tell him, and he concludes that they compose not by "wisdom" but by sheer inspiration. On the whole, Aristotle takes the same view; for him also a poem is "an inspired thing" (*Rhetoric* 3, 1408[b]19). In the *Poetics*, as we have seen, he puts this in naturalistic terms—men imitate instinctively.[67] Persons naturally endowed for these things create the art of poetry by improvisation, and as they catch glimpses of the form of tragedy, as Homer already did, they go on to realize it more and more perfectly. More by luck than art they find out the myths that embody the true tragic situations. They lose their way when they assume that the story of one man is necessarily a unity. It is poetry, not always the poets, that aims at the ethical universal; but it is wonderful how steadily the poets aim for the tragic effect or something like it. Even Homer only adumbrates dramatic form, but he is admirable beyond all other poets, since time and again he has hit upon the right procedures "whether by nature or by art" (1151[a]24). Nevertheless in this natural, half-blind process, tragedy has reached its full nature and there has stopped. Aristotle does not, of course, intend to alter poetry, but only to study it—to bring into the light of the mind exactly what tragedy, for example, is and what it exists to do, and to point out, in the light of this knowledge, the means by which a tragedy may best fulfill its tragic nature. If by "wisdom" Socrates meant conscious art, a philosopher here supplies it, should the poets care to listen. As to what their poems mean—if this means what they teach—poets could at least say that they mean nothing in that sense, but only aim to give pleasure.

A critic, and not a classical scholar, Aristotle regards the poets as his clients, not himself as theirs. He studies Poetry, not poems, Tragedy, not tragedies or tragic poets. Poems and plays are mentioned chiefly as illustrating different principles, and only a handful of poets are cited by name—among tragic poets, the fifth-century triad, Aeschylus, Sophocles, and Euripides, already canonized at this time, Agathon and Dicaeogenes, whose careers extended over the turn of the century, and three fourth-century poets, Carcinus, Astydamas, and Theodectes. Among these poets, Aeschylus is not frequently brought forward, presumably because his procedures do not represent the final development of the tragic form. Among plays, a certain prominence is given to Sophocles' *Oedipus Tyrannus* and Euripides' *Iphigenia in Tauris*, since these plays illustrate procedures that Aristotle thinks important, and also perhaps because he could count on their being familiar to his audience.

Thanks to his philosophical or scientific method, Aristotle produced a universalized theory of poetry, or at least of serious drama, that has proved remarkably applicable in times and places far removed from his own, and applicable to forms of imitation that he could not foresee. There is perhaps a certain price to pay for universalizing. We may agree that the plot, what goes on in a play, even in an "absurd" one, is of the first importance, but may still think that Character and Thought (which we tend to lump together) are too summarily dealt with in the *Poetics*. It is these elements that elevate and illuminate the plot and allow us to call a tragedy not merely competent but great; obviously they have much to do with the quality of pity and fear that the play transmits. Aristotle, however, may well have considered that what he has said of these "parts" is all that can profitably be said in a generalized account of the art. He has in fact so much to say on Thought (speeches) that he has composed a separate treatise on it, the *Rhetoric*, to which he here refers. On Character, what he says, especially in Chapters 2, 6, 9, 13, and 15, is sharply observed and much to the point. Beyond these guidelines, perhaps there is only the infinitude of individual effects that the poets' genius may discover.

In point of Thought, he notices that the recent poets make their characters speak like rhetoricians, whereas the older poets made theirs speak like statesmen. He notices also that the poets of his day, like the painters, have no interest in character drawing. It is not likely that he approves of these developments, any more than of the failure to integrate the chorus into the play. And there are other signs in the *Poetics* that fourth-century tragedy was in trouble. Though Aristotle does not say so, the instinctive tendency that he observes to limit tragedies to the few legends that embodied the sought-for tragic events must have contributed to the monotony to which he says tragedies are liable: there is a limit to the number of plots in which the same action can be represented. What Aristotle himself fears is that the familiarity of the story will make the poet careless of probability; but his generalized theory offers a remedy for both ills. Why not abandon the myths and invent entirely new actions, as Agathon did in his *Antheus*? Rationalized theory can see through the traditional material to the form; Aristotle never speaks of "heroes"—that is, the personages of legend and hence of poetry—but always of ",men," even when he describes these persons in elevated tones (13, 1453ª20). The exhaustion of the myths as the matrix of tragedy does not trouble him; and yet from the myths it would seem tragedy drew its lifeblood. Nor could this species thrive in the world that submitted to the Macedonian conqueror; it was born in the world that resisted the Persian. Though old tragedies continued to be produced in the theater, we hear of few new tragedies after the middle of the century.[68] Instead, there came forth New Comedy, entirely human, and bearing some of the features of tragedy—its peripeties and recognitions, above all its ethical universals, but always with a happy ending. We see it about to step forward in Chapter 9 of the *Poetics*.

7. *The Fortune of the* Poetics *after Aristotle*

The *Poetics*, which has played so great a part in modern thinking about literature, seems hardly to have been known at all in antiquity. Themistius (fourth century A.D.) takes from it the reference to the origin of comic plots in Sicily (*Oratio* 27, 337B from 1449ᵇ6), but it is not cited by title in any surviving writer earlier than the fifth century after Christ, when Ammonius and Boethius (fifth–sixth century) quote Chapter 20 on the "parts of speech" in their commentaries on the Aristotelian treatise *On Interpretation*.[69] Ammonius and Boethius are philosophers, and it may well be that neglect of the *Poetics* after Andronicus' edition of Aristotle was due to the departmentalization of knowledge; writers on literature and rhetoric knew only their own tradition (now almost entirely rhetorical). It is a curious fact that two writers in this department, Dionysius of Halicarnassus and Quintilian, also refer to Aristotle for the "parts of speech," but rely on his *Collection of the Art of Theodectes*, apparently in ignorance of the *Poetics*, which contains a more complete account of these parts.[70] But left so to speak in the custody of the philosophers, the

Poetics fared little better from them; there seems to have been no ancient commentary on this work. Perhaps earlier than we know, the *Poetics* as well as the *Rhetoric* may have been treated by the philosophers as a treatise on logic. Certainly, late commentators on Aristotle so regard it, probably because the *Rhetoric* and the *Poetics* followed immediately after the logical works in the corpus of Aristotle's works.[71] For example, Olympiodorus (sixth century A.D.) finds five kinds of syllogisms in Aristotle: the demonstrative, the dialectical, the rhetorical, the sophistic, and the poetic, referring for the last to the *Poetics*. The rhetorical syllogism is based on premises that are partly true and partly false, the poetic syllogism on premises that are entirely false.[72]

And yet when we read the *Epistle to the Pisos* or *Ars Poetica* of Horace, we find in it various features that strongly recall the *Poetics* of Aristotle, though these are mingled with other concerns and are scattered with the studied casualness of an epistle.[73] It is generally assumed that Horace drew these points not directly from the *Poetics* but from an intermediary source fairly close to Aristotle. This is very likely to have been the case, since the early Peripatetics, who had access to Aristotle's unpublished works, wrote extensively on literature, though unfortunately their writings are lost. Besides Theophrastus, other Peripatetics who wrote on literary subjects are Dicaearchus, Aristoxenus, Demetrius of Phalerum, Phaenias of Eresus, Satyrus, Praxiphanes, Chamaeleon, and Hieronymus of Rhodes.[74] Theophrastus himself wrote perhaps two treatises *On the Art of Poetry*, one *On Comedy*, and a very influential work *On Style*. To him the late Latin grammarian Diomedes ascribes a definition of tragedy as "a crisis (?*peristasis*) in a hero's fortunes," and the description of tragedy and comedy that follows this in Diomedes, that tragedy deals with high personages, heroes, captains, and kings, comedy with humble and private persons, may also go back to Theophrastus. It was repeated widely in antiquity and later. We may guess that in poetics as in rhetoric, the philosophical approach of Aristotle gave place in his followers to a more observational and classificatory method, but that the material and the terminology of the *Poetics* were freely used by them.[75] Porphyrion, an ancient commentator on Horace, informs us that in the *Ars Poetica* Horace "has brought together the precepts of Neoptolemus of Parium on the art of poetry—not all of them indeed but the most outstanding" (Porphyrion on Horace, *Ars Poetica* 1). Little is known of Neoptolemus, who may have lived in the first half of the third century B.C.; it has been inferred that he may have been a Peripatetic and that Horace's echoes of Aristotle may have come from him.[76] They remain echoes; Horace hardly touches on the main concerns of the *Poetics*, and he takes poetry in a broader sense, which allies it with rhetoric. His famous statement of the aims of poetry may indeed have a background in Neoptolemus: "Poets," Horace says, "wish either to bring profit or delight, or to say that which is at the same time pleasurable and suitable for life."[77]

All this is highly speculative. We might have expected an indirect tradition that brought clear echoes of the *Poetics* to Horace to have brought some echo to others as well, but this seems not to be the case.[78] It remains possible that Horace himself had glanced at the *Poetics*. This brings us to the one unequivocal use of the *Poetics* in a literary sense that survives from late antiquity. Unfortunately, it is very much of an enigma. It is a brief outline of a theory of poetry found in a tenth-century manuscript at Paris and generally called the *Tractatus Coislinianus* or anonymous *On Comedy*.[79] Its age is unknown, and it may be as late as the tenth century. The author presumably had philosophical training, since the outline (the tractate is mostly just an outline) is a logical division of *diaeresis*, the genus being Poetry. Poetry is divided into nonmimetic and mimetic; nonmimetic poetry is divided into historical and instructive; instructive poetry is divided into didactic and theoretical; mimetic poetry is divided into narrative and dramatic; dramatic poetry is divided into comedy, tragedy, mimes, and satyr dramas. Tragedy is said to remove fearful emotions from the soul through compassion and terror; to aim at a due proportion of fear; and to have grief for its mother. There follows a definition of comedy adapting word for word the definition of tragedy in the *Poetics*—e.g., "through pleasure and laughter effecting the purgation of the like emotions." "It has laughter for its mother." Laughter is then said to have two sources, the language and the "things" (= content), and each is analyzed into topics that admirably abstract the real usages of comedy. Comedy is distinguished from abuse as requiring the so-called emphasis (innuendo); it makes sport of faults of soul and body; and there should be a due proportion of laughter. The material of comedy is now said to be plot, ethos, dianoia, diction, melody, and spectacle, and each of these gets brief comment. Thus dianoia is divided into opinion and proof, and proof into oaths, compacts, testimonies, tortures, and laws. (These parts of dianoia are from Aristotle's *Rhetoric*, the writer having looked up the reference in *Poetics* 19). The quantitative parts of comedy are taken over from those of tragedy in *Poetics* 12. The tractate ends with the distinction between Old, New, and Middle comedy, which is, of course, unknown to the *Poetics*. Whether the writer, who may be excerpting a more complete work, went on to outline a theory for the other types of poetry, is uncertain but unlikely.

This compendium has been much discussed, some good scholars holding that in some way it may represent the missing part of the *Poetics* on comedy, others demurring because of the ineptitude of the definition of comedy and of the "parts" of dianoia, which, though Aristotelian, cannot be what Aristotle had in mind in the *Poetics*. The initial "division" is merely an external classification; it is not clear what the genus "poetry" is, and one could not work back to it from the subspecies. It is agreed, however, that the terminology is mostly Peripatetic and, indeed, mostly from the *Poetics*, and that the categories under the sources of laughter reflect the work of a good critic, intimately engaged with comedies. The division "from language" and "from things" is taken from Aristotle's analysis of the laughable in the *Rhetoric*, which he refers back to the *Poetics*; except that his division is "persons, language, and things," whereas the tractate, reverting to the *Poetics*, places persons under the "material" (= the six parts) of comedy. These persons—the buffoonish, the ironical, imposters—make a far better abstraction from real comedies than does the vulgar formula, "comedy deals with private persons, tragedy with kings." For the tractate, catharsis means the elimination of the passions.

This teasing document, whether late ancient or early Byzantine, remains unique in appreciating the importance of the *Poetics* for literature. What is known of the fortunes of the *Poetics* otherwise from the tenth to the fifteenth century is soon told, but at least it brings the treatise itself into view. Probably toward the end of the ninth century a translation was made into Syriac, a small portion of which remains, and from the Syriac Abú Bišer (d. 940) made an Arabic version which we have almost complete. These translations clearly were not made to promote the study of literature, but were part of the wholesale assimilation of Greek philosophy by the Arab world. On the basis of the Arabic version, the great commentator Averroes produced in Cordova in A.D. 1174 a commentary on the *Poetics*, which was known in Latin translations down to the Renaissance. Since he did not know Greek tragedy, he makes little of Aristotle's main points; he takes tragedy to be a form of encomium and in general assimilates poetics to rhetoric with a moral aim; "imitation" he takes to mean figurative expression.[80] At least, he knew that the *Poetics* was about poetry, not logic. Within the Greek world, manuscripts of the *Poetics* were at least preserved, and from the tenth or eleventh century comes the best and by far the oldest manuscript we have (Parisinus 1741).[81] But from a literary point of view there is nothing to show. In the twelfth century Joannes Tzetzes wrote extensively on comedy and tragedy, but had no knowledge of the *Poetics*. One might have expected more from the literary revival of the fourteenth century, when the ancient poets were extensively studied, and indeed our second-best and second-oldest manuscript (Riccardianus 46, in Florence) is from this period; but we hear of no use made of the treatise in literary study. In the West, the *Poetics* remained totally unknown until the thirteenth century, when Roger Bacon shows some acquaintance with Averroes's commentary in the translation of Hermannus Alemannus (A.D. 1256) (*Opus Maius*, Pt. 4). However, in 1278, William of Moerbeke, the translator-general of Aristotle for the Scholastic age, completed a Latin translation of the *Poetics*, presumably to round out his translation of the philosopher's works. It is an indication of the great change that presently came about in European culture that this translation remained unknown until 1930, when it was discovered by Père Lacombe.

There can be little doubt that the rise of Humanism in Italy in the fourteenth and fifteenth centuries brought about the most important intellectual revolution that Europe has ever experienced. Whatever other aspects this movement may have had, it succeeded in giving precedence to literary and rhetorical studies, both in the schools and in mature endeavor, over philosophical and theological interests and even professional ones. Behind the revival of letters, there was a profound, though perhaps obscure, sense of moral affinity to ancient culture. Whether the revival could have been sustained as a purely Latin movement may be doubted; as at the beginning of Latin culture and in the patristic period and again in the Scholastic period, the mother culture of Greece was indispensable, and this time, thanks to the advancing Turks, the whole of higher Greek culture, so to speak, was cast upon the shores of Italy. At no period in antiquity had Greek and Latin letters been brought together so massively as in this moment when the modern spirit was born.

In his remarkable study of the Greek manuscripts of the *Poetics*, Edgar Lobel considers twenty-nine manuscripts of this work from the fifteenth century or the first years of the sixteenth, and supposes that still others once existed. Since some of these manuscripts were copied in Greece and brought to Italy, it seems likely that the Byzantine literary revival of the fourteenth century had indeed directed attention to the treatise. The Italian Humanists, who were in general not friendly to the Aristotelian philosophical tradition, might not easily have found it out for themselves, though Petrarch was vaguely aware that it existed. Apart from these numerous manuscripts, however, little evidence has been discovered to show that the earlier Humanists attended to the *Poetics*, the first quotations from it coming from Poliziano in the 1480s. At the end of the century, it was at last given to the West in a Latin translation by Giorgio Valla, printed at Venice in 1498. Valla already had made use of the *Poetics* in his public lectures on poetry given in St. Mark's Hospital in Venice, probably sometime between 1492 and 1494.[82] It is significant that Valla knew nothing of the translation by William of Moerbeke. It is perhaps also significant that the *Poetics* and the *Rhetoric* were deliberately excluded from the great Aldine edition of Aristotle's works in 1495–1498, but were included in the first volume of the Aldine *Rhetores Graeci* in 1508. The *Poetics* was about to begin its life, for, so far as we can see, it hardly lived in antiquity or the Middle Ages, but is, so to speak, a modern book, called into life and activity by the needs of Renaissance and modern literature. These needs were not yet quite apparent at the time of Valla's translation and the first printing of the Greek text in the *Rhetores Graeci*, but became so about thirty years later. What called the *Poetics* into life was a doctrine of Imitation very different from that which it embodies. The imitation of authors was a topic belonging to the ancient tradition of rhetoric; by imitating the masters of his art, the young orator might hope to become equally proficient.[83] In the Renaissance, this doctrine rose from the textbooks of rhetoric to become a way of life. By imitating the masters of ancient literature, the modern writer would raise himself above the poverty of the preceding age. When turned from Latin to the vernacular early in the sixteenth century, the idea proved to be a powerful one and decisive for European letters for centuries to come. The object was to cultivate the vernacular so as to make it as beautiful and expressive as the ancient languages, and to introduce into it the forms of literature that in the experience of antiquity had proved to be the most adequate to meet the spiritual requirements of a high civilization. The transfer of these forms to the fertile and undepleted soil of the vernacular languages eventually produced magnificent results, but it was not easy at first. In the first decades of the century, brilliant imitations of Roman comedy were made by Ariosto and Machiavelli, rather dull tragedies by Trissino and Rucellai, and a very dull epic by Trissino; but the road leads to Shakespeare, Racine, and Milton. This movement was accompanied by a vast output of critical and theoretical writing, which existed in its own right as a disinterested and philosophical inquiry into the nature of poetry, in which the *Poetics* came to hold a central position, supplying the major topics of discussion. We see it approaching. M. A. Vida's famous *Poetica* (1527, but written earlier) does not know Aristotle; its theory is rhetorical and the moving principle imitation of authors; a new Latin translation by Pazzi appeared in 1536 and Daniello's *Poetica* of the same year shows a vague apprehension of Aristotle; we hear of unpublished discussions and lectures in the '40's, and in 1548 Robortelli published the first real commentary on the *Poetics* ever made; in 1549 Segni published the first Italian translation.

The Italian theorists were interested in Poetry, not merely in Aristotle; their fundamental tradition was rhetorical, but they gathered up all the remains of antiquity on the poetic art, and formed their own opinions. In Julius Caesar Scaliger's encyclopedic *Poetices libri septem* (1561, published in France), Aristotle is often used, but is seldom named except where Scaliger disagrees with him; he rejects the position that poetry is imitation, since his own view embraces all that goes under the name of poetry and he finds the basic principle in a peculiar use of language (i.e., his view is rhetorical). Since the restrictive *Poetics* does not supply such a general view of the aims of poetry, resort was almost universally had to Horace; but since the Renaissance was profoundly moralistic, his statement "to profit or please or both" regularly becomes "to teach delightfully," with the emphasis on teaching. These critics generally took *catharsis* as a means of moral betterment and an answer to Plato; Robortelli and others explained it by habituation—by frequently viewing the horrors of tragedy, we learn to bear our own troubles with equanimity. Minturno (1559), to be sure, interprets *catharsis* as a homeopathic cure of pity and fear, but the result of the cure is moral betterment. Castelvetro (1570) accepts this, but having probably the best understanding of Aristotle at this time, criticizes Aristotle for introducing it, since a moral purpose turns poetry into a utilitarian art serving this end; Castelvetro correctly finds pleasure alone the aim proposed by the *Poetics*. In the matter of Character, they never doubt that the personages of tragedy and epic poetry should be kings or great noblemen, those of comedy private and humble persons; they tend to translate *spoudaios* as "illustrious" (see note 12 below); they generally fail to grasp the significance of *hamartia* or tragic error in Aristotle's theory. Despite Aristotle, they regarded epic poetry as the highest type, and though agreeing that it should represent a dramatic action, demanded (Minturno, Tasso) that the epic hero be "perfect." The aim of epic poetry was to arouse moral admiration for great men. Romantic poems such as Ariosto's *Orlando* came under pressure from the classical ideal, and the resulting controversy was a kind of struggle between the Middle Ages and the classical Renaissance.[84] Even the logical interpretation of the *Poetics* was brought into play in the classification of poetry.[85]

Aristotle requires that a plot have unity of action. He notes that the action represented in tragedies seldom exceeds one revolution of the sun. In interpreting this, the theorists (Maggi, Scaliger) came to believe that for the sake of probability the action of the play should coincide in time with the stage presentation—it would be absurd for a messenger to leave for Egypt and return within an hour. It remained for Castelvetro, whose whole theory of drama is based on the fact of stage presentation, to add the requirement that the action be confined to one place, and hence to formulate the "law of the three unities"—of action, of time, and of place—that gained so much importance later. In fact, for Castelvetro the unity of action is only a corollary of the unity of place, and with this limitation tragedy can do anything that history can do. Needless to say, the three unities were unknown to Aristotle and should always be referred to Castelvetro, who invented them. The influence of the Italian critics was soon felt throughout Europe. In England, Sir Philip Sidney's *Defence of Poesie* shows direct contact with the text of the *Poetics*, but also advocates the unities of time and place and misses the importance of the unity of action; the effect of tragedy is the purification of the spectator's emotions. Shakespeare shows no knowledge of Aristotelian theory; but Ben Jonson absorbed a good deal of it, not from the Italians but from the Dutch scholar Daniel Heinsius, whose *De tragoediae constitutione* (1611) was now everywhere accepted as authoritative. Jonson understands the unity of action. In 1623 a Latin translation of the *Poetics* by Theodore Goulston appeared in London.

It was in France, however, that the Italian theorists and the *Poetics* itself had their greatest fortune in the seventeenth century both in connection with the theater and in the formation of the Neoclassical ideal of style. The names of Aristotle and Scaliger no doubt were freely invoked by many who had little real knowledge of these authors; the last edition of Scaliger was in 1617 at Heidelberg, and there was no French translation of Aristotle until 1671. Moreover, the principles most loudly proclaimed were those of the three unities, of decorum, and of *vraisemblance*, none of them strictly Aristotelian. Nevertheless, the better critics knew Aristotle well, and, what is more, the dramatists knew him. Corneille's three *Discours* (1660), in which he judges his own plays in the light of the *Poetics* and Greek tragedy, became classics in literary theory. Racine, still more of a Hellenist than Corneille, studied the *Poetics* carefully and has left interesting notes on it. The Neoclassical ideal, with its insistence on definite rules for all the literary forms, no doubt answered to a deep craving for law and order and was the counterpart in literature of the philosophy of Descartes. In 1692 André Dacier published a translation of the *Poetics* with commentary that was destined to hold the field throughout the next century: *La Poétique d'Aristote contenant les règles les plus exactes pour juger du poème héroique et des pièces de théâtre, la tragédie et la comédie*. This and a host of French critical works—e.g., René Rapin, *Reflexions sur la Poétique d'Aristote*, Abbé d'Aubignac, *Pratique du théâtre*, René Le Bossu, *Traité du poème épique*—spread throughout Europe a French Aristotle, largely replacing the Italian one. It is mostly with Dacier and Corneille that Lessing takes issue in his interpretations of Aristotle in his *Hamburgische Dramaturgie* (1767–1768).

In England, Milton had written *Samson Agonistes* (1671) in direct imitation of Greek tragedy but also with a full knowledge of Aristotle and his Italian and Dutch interpreters. In his Preface, he understands *catharsis* as a homeopathic cure whereby pity, fear or terror, and such like passions are tempered and reduced to just measure, as "in physic things of melancholic hue and quality are used against melancholy, sour against sour, salt to remove salt humors." His remarkably "modern" view of *catharsis* may have come to him from Minturno. But presently, the full force of French interpretation of Aristotle was brought to bear in England by the important critic Thomas Rymer in numerous works published between 1674 and 1713. His hilarious essay *On Probability in Othello* is still worth reading. John Dryden, though a less uncompromising Aristotelian than Rymer, belongs to the same school, declaring in his Preface to *Troilus and Cressida*[86] that he is ready to condemn his own plays when they fail to conform to Aristotle's rules. For Dryden's younger friend, the critic John Dennis, Aristotle is the lawgiver: "The Legislator of Parnassus wrote the laws of tragedy so exactly and so truly in reason and nature that succeeding critics have writ justly and reasonably upon that art no farther than they have adhered to their great master's notions."[87] On the whole, similar views continued to be held throughout the eighteenth century, though there was less inclination in England to adhere to the unities of time and place, and French influence gave way to a more direct reading of the *Poetics* itself. Addison founded his famous essays on *Paradise Lost* on the *Poetics*, and Fielding kept Aristotle before him in structuring his novels on epic principles. Samuel Johnson holds to Aristotle and is impatient of the French unities and "rules." Joseph Warton thinks Aristotle as necessary for the understanding of poetry as Euclid for attaining skill in geometry.[88] Toward the end of the century, the good English translation of Henry James Pye (1788) and the still better one by Thomas Twining (1789) found most of the English equivalents for Aristotle's terminology that we still use, and the great edition of the Greek text with commentary by Thomas Tyrwhitt (1794) surpassed all earlier editions in acuteness of observation and is still consulted with profit today.

Literary theory, which for three centuries had chiefly been dictated by the Latin nations, was profoundly altered by the new sensibility, infused with a Germanic sense of *innerlichkeit* that came to the fore in the so-called Romantic movement of the early nineteenth century. The norm of poetry seemed rather to be found in personal and lyric poetry than in drama as such, and along with a rejection of the Neoclassical "rules" as irrelevant to what poetry was now felt to be, we might well expect there to be a rejection also of the lawbook of Parnassus. But the Romantic ideal was intimately bound up with Romantic Hellenism—Shakespeare did not dethrone Homer and Sophocles—and the *Poetics*, the Greek philosopher's account of Greek poetry, continued to be held in respect, though no longer regarded as prescriptive. In particular the primacy assigned by Aristotle to plot came under attack, as in the well-known essay of John Henry Newman, "Poetry, with Reference to Aristotle's *Poetics*" (1829): "The action . . . will be more justly viewed as the vehicle for introducing the personages of the drama than as the principal object of the poet's art; it is not in the plot, but in the characters, sentiments, and diction, that the actual merit and poetry of the composition are found." The preference for character over plot, reinforced by the experience of the nineteenth-century novel, has continued until quite recently (see *Poetics*, Chapter 5, Note 15); but Newman is less interested in assigning priority to the "parts" than in discovering everywhere the manifestations of the "poetical mind," which is "imaginative and creative." These already current terms relate to the freshly apprehended concept of the organic in poetry and art, a concept that clearly springs from the *Poetics* and Plato's *Phaedrus*, but the organization is now seen not as something that *should* be there, but as something that *is* there spontaneously and inevitably as the overflow of a poetical mind. If this is so, the higher virtues of poetry cannot be predicted by any art of poetry, and can only be found by examining the individual work of art. This view, too, has prevailed, until Benedetto Croce can declare that there is no such thing as tragedy (or any other literary genre), but only the individual work of art.

Yet with all the attempt to penetrate, psychologically or anthropologically, to some inwardness of poetry, the *Poetics* has remained remarkably relevant. In the nineteenth and twentieth centuries it has been more firmly fixed in university instruction than ever before, and its terminology has been the common coin of almost all critical discussion. But to the modern mind it seems too simple and obvious to be a true account, as it stands, of either drama or narrative. Its dry sentences seem to miss the heights and depths of poetry, yet at almost every point to suggest something of far-reaching importance. It needs elucidation to recommend it to modern ways of thinking. This service was admirably performed by S. H. Butcher in the essays of his *Aristotle on Poetry and Fine Art*, first published in 1895. He accepts, for example, Bernays's account of *catharsis* as a homeopathic effect, but still describes it as purifying and ennobling the emotions; plot is more important than character, but plot springs from character; the personages should be good, but had better also be noble, and the bourgeois tragedies of Ibsen are condemned. The success of Butcher's essays suggests that the modern spirit retains certain eighteenth-century traits. The uncertainty surrounding *catharsis* has raised hopes that here was a point of escape from the matter-of-fact *technê*. The abbé Bremond thought that in *catharsis* Aristotle may have had in mind something like the abbé's own idea of mystical poetry. A revival of Heinsius's notion that *catharsis* meant ritual purification encouraged a whole school of interpreters in the belief that Aristotle had recognized the ritual and religious origins of drama that they found still operating in Greek tragedy. Those who sought to solve the puzzle of *catharsis* by observing their own reactions to tragedy might be inclined to agree with John Gassner that along with the emotional relief there went an experience of understanding and enlightment and that this was in fact the decisive element in a serious play as opposed to melodrama.[89] Gassner does not pretend that this was what Aristotle meant. Even the concept of plot, "the synthesis of the events," appears to need reinterpretation if it is to be applied significantly. R. S. Crane finds that plot must include character and thought: "The plot of any novel or drama is the particular temporal synthesis effected by the writer of the elements of action, character, and thought that constitute the matter of his invention."[90] They work together and cannot be separated. Similarly Reuben A. Brower thinks it necessary to redefine plot "as dramatic sequence perceived in the progress of meanings," which will offer "an account of literature that will do justice to its dramatic character without falling into an Aristotelian separation of plot and character from diction."[91] With Brower's essay, we are in the realm of linguistic criticism: "All structural links, large and small, from an obvious change in narrative fact to a phrasal echo, are perceived in the resonances of particular words." For this school, Aristotle's discussion of language is of minor interest; even his striking comment on metaphor, that it is most important in poetic language, that it cannot be taught but is a mark of genius, is seldom mentioned as significant. In the further development, the wedding of linguistic theory and anthropology in "structural criticism," not only tragedy but poetry itself, it seems, is annihilated in an undifferentiated view of *lexis*.[92] We are bound to recall that in antiquity also poetics seemed to vanish into a generalized account of language in Rhetoric, though in this case it was language governed by artistic aims.

From all such tentative developments, important though they may be, it is refreshing to turn back to the *Poetics* in the mood of T. S. Eliot's comment on Coleridge's theories. "For everything that Aristotle says illuminates the literature which is the occasion for saying it; but Coleridge only now and then."[93]

Notes to the Introduction

1. [On the dithyramb see *Poetics*, Chapter 1, note 2. G.M.K.]

2. ["New Comedy" is the name given to the dramatic literature which began in the last quarter of the fourth century B.C., consisting of plays of romantic adventure and bourgeois life, with much emphasis on recognitions and discoveries, usually of long-lost parents and children. The most famous poet of the New Comedy is Menander, one of whose plays is now extant in almost complete form as a result of papyrus discoveries, which have yielded also large parts of other of his plays. Other well-known poets of New Comedy include Philemon and Diphilus. G.M.K.]

3. Plutarch, *Alexander* 8 (cf. 26).

4. [The first "sin" was, of course, the execution of Socrates. G.M.K.]

5. Strabo, *Geogr.* 13.1.54; Plutarch, *Sulla* 26.

6. [Theophrastus was Aristotle's successor as head of the Lyceum, and a prolific writer of scientific treatises. His botanical works were especially esteemed. His best-known extant work is the *Characters*, a collection of thirty brief sketches of types of personality, with emphasis on human weaknesses. G.M.K.]

7. For the sake of brevity, it is convenient to use the traditional title *Poetics* for the treatise we have, though the correct title is *On the Art of Poetry*, as indicated by the opening words *Peri Poētikēs* (sc. *Technēs*).

8. A treatise *On Music* is thought to have been a mathematical study of harmonics.

9. [See Chapter 1, note 6. G.M.K.]

10 [Else, p. 483. C.M.K.]

11. [For Xenophanes, see Chapter 25, note 11. For the fragments of Heraclitus of Ephesus, a philosopher of the late sixth to early fifth century, see Kirk and Raven, *The Presocratic Philosophers* (Cambridge, 1971, pp. 182–215.]

12. To the dialogue *On Poets* modern scholars have also assigned fragment 4, Aristotle's reported statement that Plato's style was halfway between poetry and prose, and some (frg. 5) possible references to *catharsis* found in the Neoplatonic philosophers Proclus and Iamblichus.

13. The reference (Chapter 15) to a "published" work, presumably the dialogue, is good evidence that the present work was not published.

14. Some have thought that it may only represent the lecturer's private notes for expansion in delivery. But, for the most part, the thought is fully expressed. A certain special obliquity of style perhaps suggests oral composition—i.e., that it may have been dictated to an amanuensis.

15. See Lucas, *Comm.*, p. xiv, from whom this point is taken.

16. For rhetoric, see Friedrich Solmsen, *Die Entwicklung der aristotelischen Logik und Rhetorik* (Berlin, 1929), pp. 196–229; for the *Poetics*, see Solmsen's article cited in the Introduction, note 20.

17. Cross references in the *Rhetoric* to the *Poetics* are put in the past tense, and for unpublished lecture materials this seems more likely to indicate prior delivery than prior composition. The single reference in the *Poetics* to the *Rhetoric* (*Poet.* 19, 1456^{a}35) is temporally ambiguous. The reference to the *Poetics* for catharsis in the *Politics* (8, 1341^{b}38) in the future tense seems more likely to refer to a coming lecture than to a work not yet in being; cf. Lucas *Comm.*, p. xiv.

18. Quintilian, *Institutes of Oratory*, 3, 1, 14, where it seems to be implied that the afternoon lectures were open to the public; cf. Gellius, *Attic Nights* 20.20.

19. Diogenes Laertius, *Arist.* 1 (5.1).

20. For what may be early and what late in the *Poetics*, see Friedrich Solmsen, "The Origins and Methods of Aristotle's *Poetics*," *CQ* 29 (1935):192–201, reprinted in *Kleine Schriften* V. 2, pp. 119–128, and Daniel de Montmollin, *La Poetique d'Aristotle* (Neuchatel, 1951). Cf. Else, pp. xi, 667–669 (for an index of his discussions of individual passages).

21. *Poet.* 6, 1450^{a}l; 17, 1455^{b}7; 18, 1455^{b}32; 23, 1459^{b}5, 7; 26, 1462^{a}16.

22. Cf. Lucas, *Comm.*, p. xv. For a list of works touching on poetry before and during the time of Aristotle, see Alfred Gudeman, "The Sources of Aristotle's *Poetics*," in *Classical Studies in Honor of John C. Rolfe*, ed. G. D. Hadzsits (Philadelphia, 1931), pp. 75–100.

23. Besides Aristotle, the only one of Plato's pupils who seems to have written extensively on poetry is Heraclides of Pontus. Among the titles ascribed to him by Diogenes Laertius (*Arist.*, V, 87–88) are *On the Art of Poetry and on Poets* in one book, *On the Three Tragic Poets* in one book, and *Solutions of Homeric Problems* in two books. From this last we have some quotations—it was similar to Aristotle's *Homeric Problems*—but unfortunately nothing is known of the others.

24. [Gorgias of Leontini, Sicily, was a famous theorist and practitioner of rhetoric, with whose arrival in Athens in 427 the Athenian development of prose style is closely associated. G.M.K.]

25. *Apate* has been compared with the false utterances the Muses can make. Hesiod, *Theog.* 26–28.

26. The explanation presumably is due to Plutarch, who quotes the saying of Gorgias (*On the Fame of the Athenians* 5, p. 348C).

27. The anonymous author of the *Dissoi Logoi* (Diels, *Vorsokratiker*[6] 2.90).

28. On Plato and imitation, see W. J. Verdenius, *Mimesis: Plato's Doctrine of Artistic Imitation and Its Meaning to Us* (Leiden: E. J. Brill, 1949).

29. In Plato's view they abuse a good principle. Properly, imitation is the reproduction of a model and its virtues are correctness and truth telling; the world is good insofar as it correctly imitates the ideas. See Richard McKeon, "Literary Criticism and the Concept of Imitation in Antiquity," in *Critics and Criticism*, ed. R. S. Crane (Chicago, 1952).

30. See Richard Robinson, *Definition* (Oxford, 1950).

31. *Metaphysics* 1025^{b}25.

32. *An. Post.* 2.13, 96^{b}15 (Oxford translation, adapted). Essential properties or attributes are defined by Aristotle as properties not mentioned in the definition of a thing but necessarily deduced from it (*Metaphysics* 4.30, 1025^{a}30). His favorite example is that from the definition of triangle it is necessarily deduced that the angles are equal to two right angles.

33. For the definition of "part," see *Metaphysics* 5.25, 1023^{b}12–^{b}26. 1023^{b}23–^{b}26 is the most apposite definition (dealing with parts of definition) to our discussion.

34. *An. Post.* 1.28, 87^{a}38.

35. Species alone can have "parts" and "essential properties." For genus and *differentiae* as "first things," see p. 45 of trans. (1447^{a}12). A different interpretation of this passage is given by Ross (in *Prior and Posterior Analytics* on *An. Post.* 1.28, 87^{a}38).

36. It has been complained that Aristotle does not in fact discuss the art of poetry "in general," but, as we have seen, the discussion of the species *is* the discussion of the genus, the genus having no existence apart from its species. Actually, only individual poems or plays exist in reality, but there is no science of individual things unless they are classified—e.g., as poems or plays.

37. Aristotle has legitimately raised the genus "art of poetry" to the higher genus "imitation." To take it the other way round—imitative poetry as a subgenus of poetry—would be possible and might seem more natural, "poetry" (making) then being taken in turn as a subgenus of "art" (cf. Plato, *Symposium* 205 B10–C11) and imitation as a *differentia*. But *imitation* is naturally the wider term, since (Chapter 4) it is the source of the art of poetry and of other things as well.

38. See p. 22 and note 67. Aristotle's pupils would recognize here a familiar tenet, formulated in the *Physics* (2.1, 193^{b}12) as "Nature in the sense of genesis is the way to nature."

39. First the *fact* is proved through signs (we enjoy imitations even of unpleasant things) and then the *reasoned fact* through causes (because reading imagery is a form of learning). See *An. Pr.* 2.27, 70^{a}3 ff., and *An. Post.* 1.13, 78^{a}23 ff.

40. The language echoes Plato's words for this process in *Phaedrus* 265D.

41. *An. Post.* 73^{a}26. *Poet.* 6, 1450^a, 12–14.

42. To be sure, in the context the statement, "the plot is the imitation of the action," may be understood as "of a serious action," but Aristotle does not wish the parts in themselves to have qualities. The parts are attributes of tragedy as drama not as tragedy, just as the attribute "having angles equal to two right angles" belongs to isosceles triangles as triangles not as isosceles (*An. Post.* 73^{b}38).

43. The "parts" of animals are also essential attributes (*Part. An.* 1.5, 645^{b}1) and constituent elements (*Part. An.* 2.1, 646^{a}8, cf. *Poet.* 1447^{a}10). The essential parts of tragedy are perhaps analogous to the "uniform parts" of animals (flesh, blood, bones, etc.), and if so, the quantitive parts (prologue, episodes, etc.) are perhaps inevitably introduced (Chapter 12) as corresponding to

the "nonuniform parts" of animals (face, hands, etc.) that give an animal species its recognizable *schema* or outward appearance.

44. Cf. *Part. An.* 1.5, 645^{b}19: "In some way the body exists for the sake of the soul, and the parts of the body for the sake of those functions to which they are severally adapted."

45. Such properties do not indicate essence: *Topics* 102^{a}18 (but see Ross's footnote on *idion*, *An. Post.* 1.3, 73^{a}7).

46. However, Aristotle's language here recalls that of his logical works, and it is not irrelevant to note that the syllogism is also a *logos* having beginning, middle, and end, and the rhetorical syllogism or "enthymeme" is one that leads from a probable beginning to a probable conclusion (*An. Pr.* 2.27, 70^{b}3 ff.; *Rhet.* 1.2, 1357^{a}22 ff.

47. We easily assume that what usually happens always happens; cf. *Topics*, *loc. cit.*

48. *An. Pr.* 2.27, 70^{a}4 (Oxford tr.).

49. The marvelous, which basically is the improbable or absurd, is also a desirable dramatic and narrative quality, but it is most effectively used when the marvelous event conceals a hidden probability (Chapters 9 and 24).

50. Cf. *Rhet.* 1.2, 1357^{a}36: "In relation to what it refers to, the probable stands as the universal to the particular."

51. In earlier chapters, either ending is contemplated as apparently acceptable. Chapter 13 may have been added later than Chapter 14.

52. Solmsen, *CQ* (1935) (see above, note 20). However, some of the items may be early; practical observations and advice are likely to have been offered in the "arts" of rhetoric of which Aristotle made a collection, and if the *Poetics* is the first "art" of poetry (Lucas, *Comm.*, p. xv), it may well preserve this feature from these earlier *technai*. This section could not have been placed usefully anywhere but here, between plot/character and thought/language.

53. Aristotle first turns to language in Chapter 19, where he dismisses the distinguishing of different types of sentences as not germane to the poet's art, though he may originally have intended to pursue it (see Chapter 19, note 4). Chapter 20 is a study of basic language which seems even less relevant since it is apparently founded on the Platonic *diaeresis* and, indeed, recalls the diaeretical treatment of language in Plato's *Philebus*; it may be an early effort retained here as a general introduction to the subject (see Chapter 20, note 1).

54. The Greek word *lexis* covers both language in general and a particular language or style.

55. See *Rhet.* 3.2, 1404^{b}25.

56. Aristotle constantly seeks to reduce complexes to a finite number. Sometimes the number seems to be demonstrated—two causes for the birth of poetry, six parts of tragedy—but at other times we are left to assume that he has exhaustively divided a given area from a given point of view—four points to be observed about character, four types of tragedy.

57. Is its use here perhaps carried over from the *Homeric Problems?*

58. Scholars have been puzzled to find a place in the *Poetics* where the subject of *catharsis* might logically have been introduced, since the *Politics* promises that it will be discussed here. Aristotle may have been similarly puz-

zled and may have abandoned the notion of adding it, though he let the *Politics* passage (1341ᵇ38) stand. *Catharsis* has to do with the spectator's emotional nature rather than with the poet's procedures, which are the concern of the *Poetics*.

59. See Chapter 6, note 4.

60. W. D. Ross, *Aristotle*² (London, 1930), pp. 123–128, 237.

61. In our view of character, the tragic error and the ethical universal are essential services of character to plot, but Aristotle seems to think of them only as elements of plot.

62. E.g., Plato, *Rep.* 2.18–21, 10.8; *Laws* 392; *Phaedrus* 264B–E, 268D.

63. *Pol.* 1339ᵇ; 1341ᵇ.

64. The sophistic speaker imitates justice ignorantly (*Sophist* 267–268); poets persuade insidiously (*Republic* 10.8). Tragic poets are rhetoricians, flattering the multitude (*Gorgias* 502A–B, *Republic* 10.8); poets influence us (*Republic* 606A–B).

65. See the analysis of the emotions in the second book of Aristotle's *Rhetoric*, which includes pity and fear, and compare the *Poetics*, Chapter 19, 1456ᵇ1, on rhetoric, where anger is added to pity and fear. It may be in point to note that in Plato's *Phaedrus* (267C–D), in a context considering both rhetoric and poetry, an aspiring dramatist is represented as boasting of his ability to compose speeches expressing precisely these two emotions.

66. Conceivably, the expression "more philosophical and a higher thing than history" might be aimed at the school of Isocrates, where history may have been a subject for study, as apparently it was not in the Academy.

67. Our word "instinct" is a reduction of the scholastic phrase *instinctu naturae*, "by an impulse of nature," in which the operative word is "nature"; instinct means no more, therefore, than Aristotle's favorite term *phusei*, "by nature."

68. See A. Pickard-Cambridge, *The Dramatic Festival of Athens*, 2d ed. (Oxford, 1968) pp. 81–82.

69. The story of Mitys' statue (1452ᵃ8) is repeated in the pseudo-Aristotelian *De mirabilibus auscultationibus* 846ᵃ, also a very late work; in a different form, probably not dependent on the *Poetics*, it also appears in Plutarch, *Moralia* 553D. References to Ammonius and Boethius may be found in Bywater, Comm., pp. 261–62.

70. Dionys. Hal., *Composition of Words* 2, p. 8 R; Quint., *Inst. Orat.* 1, 4, 18. Rosc, p. 114.

71. For Diogenes Laertius (third century A.D.?), Aristotle's logic has two aims, either probability or truth; "for each of these he employed two faculties—dialectic and rhetoric where the aim is probability, analytic and philosophy where the aim is truth." Poetics is not mentioned, but it might be easy to add it to rhetoric, since it, too, aims at probability. Aristotle himself begins his *Rhetoric* with the statement that rhetoric is the counterpart of dialectic.

72. See Richard Walzer, "Zur Traditionsgeschichte der aristotelischen Poetik," *Studi italiani di filologia classica* N.S. 11 (1934):5–14.

73. Thus Horace chiefly considers epic and dramatic poetry, not the types of poetry that he himself wrote; he thinks of the poet as an imitator of life

(v. 318); the iambic meter is suitable for dialogue (81); the beginning, middle, and end of a poem must harmonize (152); the poet must either portray traditional personages or invent new ones, in the latter case taking care to make them self-consistent (119-127); the personages must be endowed with the proper emotions and weep if we are to weep with them (110-111); certain things—e.g., Procne changing into a bird—cannot credibly be staged (185-188); a god ("from the machine") should not intervene unnecessarily (191); the chorus should play the part of an actor and not merely sing interludes between the acts (193-195); the epic poet should follow Homer's method and not begin the Trojan War from the birth of Helen (147). Since the *Ars Poetica* can be roughly divided between topics concerning the poem and topics concerning the poet, it is often assumed that Aristotle's *Poetics* and dialogue *On Poets* are in the background of this division.

74. Heraclides of Pontus, Aristotle's contemporary and a member of the Academy, wrote *On Poetics and the Poets*, a title that suggests an allusion to Aristotle's two works, and it has been surmised that it may have been written in answer to Aristotle (Fritz Wehrli, *Heraclides Ponticus* [Basle, 1953], pp. 119-120).

75. A papyrus fragment of Satyrus' *Life of Euripides* (*Oxyr. Pap.* IX, p. 149, frg. 39, 7) shows him using the words "peripety" and "recognitions"; another papyrus fragment of an unknown writer (see Lucas, *Comm.*, p. 159), besides using the terms *lexis, ethos,* and *dianoia,* treats of "the suitable" (*homoios*) in a way that possibly alludes to *Poetics* 1454^{a}24. The comic poet Menander uses "recognition" in what seems to be a technical sense, *The Arbitrants* 1121. From the Peripatetics, if not from the *Poetics* itself, some of this terminology seems to have passed to the literary scholars of Alexandria in the third century and so into the biographies of the poets, arguments to plays, and scholia.

76. The case is impressively argued by C. O. Brink in his *Horace on Poetry,* Parts I and II (Cambridge, 1963, 1971), who thinks that Neoptolemus drew not only on the *Poetics* but also on the *Rhetoric* and the dialogue *On Poets;* but see the critique by Gordon Williams in the *Journal of Roman Studies* 54 (1964):186-96.

77. Horace A. P., 333-334. Neoptolemus seems to have used the word *psychagogia.* (Cf. Brink, *Horace on Poetry,* 352.) However, the question whether poetry only pleases (moves) or also teaches was at least as old as Hesiod and is the basis of Plato's objections; for music, it yields Aristotle's division in the *Politics* between music that is educational, or produces catharsis, or mere pleasure. Eratosthenes (third century B.C.) contended that poetry only "aims at pleasure (psychagogia), not instruction (didascalia)," a position vigorously contested by Strabo in his well-known defense of Homer (*Geog.* 1.3). The word *psychagogia* is very often used to indicate the aim or effect of poetry (see LSJ, s.v.), and is used by Aristotle (*Poet.* 6, 1450^{a}34). It is close to Gorgias' *apate.*

78. The attempt of A. Rostagni to find a widespread influence of the *Poetics* in antiquity has found little favor ("Aristotele e l'aristotelismo nella storia dell'estetica antica," *Stud. Ital. di Filologia Classica* 2 (1922):1-147; *Scritti minori* (Turin, 1955), 1.76-254).

79. An English translation, followed by literary illustrations, will be found in Lane Cooper, *An Aristotelian Theory of Comedy* (New York, 1922), pp. 224-286.

80. See Bernard Weinberg, *A History of Literary Criticism in the Italian Renaissance* (Chicago, 1961), I, 352-361. Averroes also produced a shorter commentary, the *Epitome*.

81. It is indicative of the interest of the age that the *Poetics* is grouped in the Paris manuscript with more than a dozen rhetorical works by authors such as Dionysius of Halicarnassus, Demetrius, Aelius Aristides, and Apsines as well as Aristotle's own *Rhetoric*. Perhaps the most accessible list of the contents of Parisinus 1741 will be found in R. Kassel, *Der Text der aristotelischen Rhetorik* (Berlin: De Gruyter, 1971), pp. 10-11.

82. See E. N. Tigerstedt, "Observations on the Reception of the Aristotelian *Poetics* in the Latin West," *Studies in the Renaissance* 15 (1968):7-24. The substance of Valla's lectures was published in his posthumous *De expetendis ac fugiendis rebus opus* (Venice: Aldus, 1501).

83. Quint., *Inst. Orat.* X, 5.19

84. Ariosto, however, proceeding from mere imitation, had successfully pivoted his poem on the madness of Orlando as the *Iliad* is pivoted on the wrath of Achilles. Tasso, whose *Gerusalemme* is molded by literary theory, makes his ostensible hero, Goffredo, "perfect," but is obliged to draw the dramatic action from a "flawed" hero, Rinaldo.

85. See the quotations from Benedetto Varchi and Jacopo Mazzoni in Allan H. Gilbert, *Literary Criticism, Plato to Dryden* (Philadelphia: Richard West, 1978), pp. 367 ff.; also Tasso, in Weinberg, I, 33.

86. *Essays of John Dryden*, ed. W. P. Ker (Oxford, 1900), p. 207.16-25.

87. Herrick, p. 82.

88. Herrick, p. 133.

89. John Gassner, "Catharsis and the Modern Theater" (1937), in *Aristotle's "Poetics" and English Literature*, ed. Elder Olson (Chicago, 1965), pp. 108-113.

90. R. S. Crane, "The Concept of Plot and the Plot of *Tom Jones*," in *Critics and Criticism*, p. 66. Crane believes the meaning of Aristotle to be that Plot governs and organizes Character, Character in turn governs and organizes Thought, and Thought finally governs and organizes Diction, the lower elements being the material of the next higher ones, and all ultimately being formed by Plot. This seems to be more Aristotelian than Aristotle.

91. Reuben A. Brower, "The Heresy of Plot," in *Aristotle's "Poetics" and English Literature*, pp. 157-174.

92. See Paul de Man, "The Crisis of Contemporary Criticism," *Arion* 6 (1967):38-57.

93. T. S. Eliot, "The Perfect Critic," in *The Sacred Wood: Essays on Poetry and Criticism* (New York: Methuen, 1961), p. 13.

The Poetics

A Note on the Translation

The translation has been made with all the modern commentaries at hand. It has been gone through finally with Kassel's Oxford text. I have preferred my own conjectures at 1449ᵇ37: τούτους (*toutous*) for οὕς (*hous*) (ms.); and at 1456ᵇ8: ἰδίᾳ (*idiâi*) for ἡδέα (*hêdea*) (ms.).

[Hutton intended to publish, in a separate article, his arguments for these two readings, but left no notes on them. In favor of τούτους is its improvement of the syntax of the passage. ἰδίᾳ ("independently," "on their own") is idiomatically sound and is a less violent change from the corrupt MS reading than Vahlen's conjecture ᾗ δέοι (*hêi deoi*, "as they should"), which most editors and translators accept. Hutton's reading gains probability from the fact that *eta* and *iota* were frequently confused in late Antiquity and the Middle Ages, as they are in modern Greek. G.M.K.]

1. The Mimetic Arts

The art of poetry, both in its general nature and in its various specific forms, is the subject here proposed for discussion. And with regard
to each of the poetic forms, I wish to consider what characteristic
effect it has, how its plots should be constructed if the poet's work is to
be good, and also the number and nature of the parts of which the
form consists. Such other matters as may be relevant to this field of
study will likewise be included. Let us, then, follow the order of nature,
and begin by taking up that which is by nature first.[1]

The basic principle: imitation. Epic poetry and Tragedy, also Comedy,
the Dithyramb,[2] and most of the music performed on the flute and the
lyre[3] are all, in a collective sense, Imitations.[4] However, they differ
from one another in three ways—either (1) by using different means [or
media] of imitation; or (2) by imitating different objects; or (3) by
imitating in a different manner and not in the same mode of presentation.

Differences based on the means of imitation. Just as certain persons, by
rule of art or mere practice, make likenesses of various objects by
imitating them in colors and forms, and others again imitate by means
of the voice, so, taken as a whole, the arts I have mentioned have as
their means of imitation rhythm, language, and melody. These, however, they employ either separately or in combination. For example,
the arts of the flutist and citharist employ only rhythm and melody, as
do other arts of similar effect such as that of the panpipes; and rhythm
alone without melody is the medium of the dance—dancers simply by
means of a rhythmical pattern of movement succeed in imitating men's
characters, emotions, and actions.

The art that imitates in language alone, in prose or in [nonlyrical]
verse (whether combining different meters or using only one of them),
remains to this day without a name.[5] For there is no common name
under which we can bring the prose mimes of Sophron and Xenarchus
and the Socratic dialogues,[6] nor would there be even if the imitation
they embody were made in iambic trimeters, elegiac couplets, or any
other such verse—except, indeed, that people in general attach the
word "poet" to the name of a particular meter and speak, for example,
of elegiac poets and epic poets, calling them poets, not on the basis of
imitation, but indiscriminately according to the meter they use.[7] This
is customary even when what is produced is a versified treatise on
medicine or natural science. But Homer and Empedocles have nothing
in common except just their meter, and it is right, therefore, to call the
one a poet and the other a physical philosopher rather than a poet.[8]

45

Similarly, anyone who produces an imitation, even if it is in a mixture of all the verse forms, as in the case of Chaeremon's *Centaur*, which is a mixed rhapsody in all the meters, must in virtue of his imitation be called a poet.[9] In these matters, then, the distinctions thus made may suffice.

There are, however, certain arts that make use of all the stated media, viz., rhythm, song, and metrical language, and among these are dithyrambic poetry, nomic poetry,[10] tragedy, and comedy. Here the distinction is that dithyramb and nome employ all three media continuously throughout, while tragedy and comedy employ first one means and then the other.[11]

This completes what I have to say about the differences among the arts in respect to the means they employ in effecting the imitation.

2. Differences Arising from the Objects of Imitation

1448[a] Since the objects that the imitators represent are persons engaged in action, and since these persons will necessarily be persons of either a higher or a lower moral type (for this is the one division that characters submit to almost without exception, goodness and badness being universal criteria of character), they represent them accordingly as either better than we are or worse or about the same.[1] For example, among painters, Polygnotus portrayed men better than we are, Pauson men inferior to the norm, and Dionysius men like ourselves.[2] And clearly, each of the aforementioned kinds of imitation will have these variations, and will be different by virtue of imitating objects that differ in this way. Thus it is possible for these differences to arise in dancing and in flute and lyre playing, and also in the art that employs prose and unsung verse. Homer, for example, represents men better than we are, Cleophon men like ourselves, and Hegemon of Thasos, the inventor of parodies, and Nicochares, author of the *Deilaid*, men worse than the norm.[3] Similarly, one could represent different types in dithyrambs and nomes, as . . . Timotheus and Philoxenus do in their treatment of the Cyclops.[4] And it is upon the same point of difference also that tragedy parts company with comedy, since comedy prefers to imitate persons who are worse, tragedy persons who are better, than the present generation.[5]

3. Differences in the Manner of Imitating

The third difference in these arts has to do with the manner in which any one of these objects may be imitated; for it is possible to represent the same objects in the same medium but in different modes. Thus they may be imitated either in narration (whether the narrator speaks at times in an assumed role, which is Homer's way, or always in his own person without change) or in a mode in which all the characters are presented as functioning and in action.[1]

It is in these three ways, then, as we said at the beginning, that imitation is differentiated—by the means, by the objects, and by the manner of presentation. So in one way Sophocles would be the same kind of imitator as Homer, in that both represent noble characters, and in another way the same as Aristophanes, since both present their characters as acting and doing (*prattontes* and *drôntes*).

A note suggested by "acting and doing." Indeed, some say that dramas are so called, because their authors represent the characters as "doing" them (*drôntes*).[2] And it is on this basis that the Dorians lay claim to the invention of both tragedy and comedy. For comedy is claimed by the Megarians here in Greece, who say it began among them at the time when they became a democracy,[3] and by the Megarians of Sicily on the grounds that the poet Epicharmus came from there and was much earlier than Chionides and Magnes;[4] while tragedy is claimed by certain Dorians of the Peloponnese. They offer the words as evidence, noting that outlying villages, called *dêmoi* by the Athenians, are called *kômai* by them, and alleging that *kômôdoi* (comedians) acquired their name, not from *kômazein* (to revel), but from the fact that, being expelled in disgrace from the city, they wandered from village to village. The Dorians further point out that their word for "to do" is *drân*, whereas the Athenians use *prattein*.[5]   1448[b]

Let this be our account, then, of the number and nature of the differences imitation admits of.

4. The Origin of Poetry and the Growth of Drama

For the beginnings of poetry in general, there appear to have been two causes, both rooted in human nature.[1] Thus from childhood it is instinctive in human beings to imitate, and man differs from the other animals as the most imitative of all and getting his first lessons by imitation, and by instinct also all human beings take pleasure in imitations. We have evidence of this in actual experience, for the forms of those things that are distressful to see in reality—for example, the basest animals and corpses—we contemplate with pleasure when we find them represented with perfect realism in images.[2] For this again the reason is that the experience of learning things is highly enjoyable, not only for philosophers but for other people as well, only their share in it is limited; when they enjoy seeing images, therefore, it is because *contrast w/*

Plato

as they look at them they have the experience of learning and reasoning out what each thing represents, concluding, for example, that "this figure is so and so"; for if the image depicts something one has not seen before, the pleasure it gives will not be that of an imitation but will come from its workmanship or coloring or some other such source. Imitation, then, being something that we have by nature, and the same being true of melody and rhythm (verses clearly are segments of the various rhythms), at the outset, persons who had a special aptitude for these things, making improvements bit by bit, produced out of their improvisations the beginnings of poetry.[3]

And in accordance with their individual types of character, poetry split into two kinds; for the graver spirits tended to imitate noble actions and noble persons performing them, and the more frivolous poets the doings of baser persons, and as the more serious poets began by composing hymns and encomia, so these began with lampoons. To be sure, we cannot mention any poem of this type by a pre-Homeric poet, though doubtless many composed them, but beginning with Homer we can—his own *Margites*,[4] for example, among other similar works. In these invectives the iambic meter came into use as something suited to their character[5]—in fact, we now call this particular meter iambic because it was the meter in which men lampooned (iambized) one another.

Thus among the early poets, some became poets of heroic verse and others again of iambic verse. Homer was not only the master poet of the serious vein, unique in the general excellence of his imitations and especially in the dramatic quality he imparts to them, but was also the first to give a glimpse of the idea of comedy by avoiding personal abuse and giving dramatic treatment to the ridiculous; for his *Margites*[6] is analogous to the comedies just as the *Iliad* and the *Odyssey* are to the tragedies. And once tragedy and comedy had made their appearance, those who were drawn to one or the other of the branches of poetry, true to their natural bias, became either comic poets instead of iambic poets or tragic poets instead of epic poets because the new types were more important—i. e., got more favorable attention, than the earlier ones.[7]

1449[a]

Whether tragedy has, then, fully realized its possible forms or has not yet done so is a question the answer to which both in the abstract and in relation to the audience [or the theater] may be left for another discussion.[8] Its beginnings, certainly, were in improvisation, as were also those for comedy, tragedy originating in impromptus by the leaders of the dithyrambic chorus, and comedy in those of the leaders of the phallic performances which still remain customary in many cities.[9] Little by little tragedy grew greater as the poets developed whatever they perceived of its emergent form, and after passing through many changes, it came to a stop, being now in possession of its specific nature.

It was Aeschylus who first[10] increased the number of the actors from one to two and reduced the role of the chorus, giving first place to the dialogue.[11] Sophocles [added] the third actor and [introduced] painted scenery. Again, [there was a change] in magnitude; from little plots and ludicrous language (since the change was from the satyr play), tragedy came only late in its development to assume an air of dignity, and its meter changes from the trochaic tetrameter to the iambic trimeter.[12] Indeed, the reason why they used the tetrameter at first was that their form of poetry was satyric [i.e., for "satyrs"] and hence more oriented toward dancing; but as the spoken parts developed, natural instinct discovered the appropriate meter, since of all the metrical forms the iambic trimeter is best adapted for speaking. (This is evident, since in talking with one another we very often utter iambic trimeters, but seldom dactylic hexameters, or if we do we depart from the tonality of normal speech.[13] Again, [there was a change] in the number of episodes[14]—but as for this and the way in which reportedly each of the other improvements came about, let us take it all as said, since to go through the several details would no doubt be a considerable task.

5. Notes on Comedy, Epic Poetry, and Tragedy

Comedy, as we have said, is an imitation of persons worse than the average. Their badness, however, does not extend to the point of utter depravity; rather, ridiculousness is a particular form of the shameful and may be described as the kind of error and unseemliness that is not painful or destructive. Thus, to take a ready example, the comic mask is unseemly and distorted but expresses no pain.[1]

(While the changes marking the development of tragedy, and the persons responsible for them, did not pass unnoticed, no attention was paid to comedy in its early stages because comedy was not regarded as important; only rather late in its history did the archon begin granting a chorus of comedians, the performers having previously been volunteers.[2] Thus when there begins to be any record of comic poets, so designated, comedy already possessed its general outlines, and we do not know who introduced masks or prologues or the accepted number of actors or anything of that sort. However, the practice of composing comic plots originally came from Sicily,[3] and in Athens Crates[4] was the first to discard the abusive mode and construct a universalized type of plot or fable.)

1449b

Epic poetry followed[5] tragedy to the extent of being an imitation of good men in the medium of metrical language; where they differ is in the narrative manner of epic and its use of a single meter. There is also a difference in length: tragedy endeavors as far as possible to keep within one revolution of the sun, or to exceed this limit but little, whereas the epic is without restriction as to time and herein differs from tragedy, although at first the treatment of time in tragedies was just the same as in epic poems.[6] Their constituent parts are the same, except that there are two [Music and Spectacle] which are peculiar to tragedy; and consequently anyone who knows how to distinguish good tragedy from bad can do the same with epic, since tragedy has all the parts that epic has, but epic not all those that make up tragedy.

6. Tragedy Defined and Analyzed into Parts

The mimetic art in hexameters [epic poetry] and comedy will be discussed later on; but at this point I wish to speak about tragedy and to begin by gathering up from what I have already said the definition of its nature that emerges from that.[1] Thus, Tragedy is an imitation of an action that is serious,[2] complete, and possessing magnitude; in embellished language, each kind of which is used separately in the different parts;[3] in the mode of action and not narrated; and effecting through pity and fear [what we call] the *catharsis* of such emotions.[4] By "embellished language" I mean language having rhythm and melody, and by "separately in different parts" I mean that some parts of a play are carried on solely in metrical speech while others again are sung.

The constituent parts of tragedy. Since the imitation is carried out in the dramatic mode by the personages themselves, it necessarily follows, first, that the arrangement of Spectacle will be a part of tragedy,[5] and next, that Melody and Language will be parts, since these are the media in which they effect the imitation. By "language" I mean precisely the composition of the verses, by "melody" only that which is perfectly obvious.[6] And since tragedy is the imitation of an action and is enacted by men in action, these persons[7] must necessarily possess certain qualities of Character and Thought, since these are the basis for our ascribing qualities to the actions themselves—character and thought are two natural causes of actions—[8]and it is in their actions that men universally meet with success or failure. The imitation of the action is the Plot. By plot I here mean the combination of the events;[9] Character is that in virtue of which we say that the personages are of such and such a quality; and Thought is present in everything in their utterances that aims to prove a point or that expresses an opinion.

1450[a]

Necessarily, therefore, there are in tragedy as a whole, considered as a special form, six constituent elements, viz. Plot, Character, Language, Thought, Spectacle, and Melody. Of these elements, two [Language and Melody] are the *media* in which they effect the imitation, one [Spectacle] is the *manner*, and three [Plot, Character, Thought] are the *objects* they imitate; and besides these there are no other parts. So then they employ these six forms, not just some of them so to speak;[10] for every drama has spectacle, character, plot, language, melody, and thought in the same sense, but the most important of them is the organization of the events [the plot].

Plot and character. For tragedy is not an imitation of men but of actions and of life. It is in action that happiness and unhappiness are found, and the end we aim at is a kind of activity, not a quality;[11] in accordance with their characters men are of such and such a quality, in accordance with their actions they are fortunate or the reverse. Consequently, it is not for the purpose of presenting their characters that the agents engage in action, but rather it is for the sake of their actions that they take on the characters they have. Thus, what happens—that is, the plot—is the end for which a tragedy exists, and the end or purpose is the most important thing of all. What is more, without action there could not be a tragedy, but there could be without characterization. In fact, the tragedies of most of our recent playwrights are lacking in the ethical element, and generally speaking many poets [of all kinds] show a similar tendency. So too among painters, Zeuxis stands in contrast with Polygnotus, the latter being an excellent portrayer of character, whereas there is no delineation of character at all in the painting of Zeuxis.[12] And again, merely by stringing together a succession of speeches full of character and well composed in point of language and thought, one will never create the effect we said was proper to tragedy, but this effect is much more apt to be achieved with a tragedy possessing a plot and coordinated events, even though it may be relatively deficient in its treatment of these other elements.[13] A further point: the principal means by which tragedy exerts its fascination are parts of the plot, that is to say reversals and recognitions.[14] Finally, it is significant that beginning authors are able to attain proficiency in language and character portrayal sooner than in plot construction—a point that may also be illustrated from nearly all the early dramatists. Clearly, then, the first principle and, as it were, the soul of tragedy is the plot, and second in importance is character. In painting, too, it is much the same—a painter who smeared on the most beautiful colors at random would give less pleasure than he would by making a likeness of something in black and white. Tragedy is an imitation of an action, and it is an imitation of the agents chiefly owing to the action.[15]

1450b

Thought. Third in order of importance comes the element of Thought. This is the ability to say what it is possible and appropriate to say [on any subject], which in oratory is the function of the arts of statesmanship and rhetoric. [I name both], since the early poets made their personages speak in the manner of statesmen, whereas those of our time make theirs speak rhetorically. [Thought must be distinguished from Character.] "Character" is whatever reveals a person's habit of moral choice—whatever he tends to choose or reject when the choice is not obvious[16]—and this element is, therefore, absent from speeches in which there is absolutely no choosing or rejecting of anything by the speaker. "Thought," on the other hand, is present whenever speakers are engaged in proving that something is so or not so, or when they are making some general pronouncement.

Language, melody, spectacle. The fourth element is Language. I define Language, as I said earlier,[17] to be the expression of meaning by the use of words, and the definition is as valid for verse as for prose. Of the remaining elements, Melody is the most important of the pleasurable accessories, while Spectacle, though fascinating in itself, is of all the parts the least technical in the sense of being least germane to the art of poetry. For tragedy fulfills its function even without a public performance and actors, and, besides, in the realization of the spectacular effects the art of the property man counts for more than the art of the poets.[18]

7. The Plot: Completeness and Magnitude

Now that the parts are established, let us next discuss what qualities the plot should have, since plot is the primary and most important part of tragedy. I have posited that tragedy is an imitation of an action that is a whole and complete in itself and of a certain magnitude—for a thing may be a whole, and yet have no magnitude to speak of. Now a thing is a whole if it has a beginning, a middle, and an end. A beginning is that which does not come necessarily after something else, but after which it is natural for another thing to exist or come to be. An end, on the contrary, is that which naturally comes after something else, either as its necessary sequel or as its usual [and hence probable] sequel, but itself has nothing after it. A middle is that which both comes after something else and has another thing following it. A well-constructed plot, therefore, will neither begin at some chance point nor end at some chance point, but will observe the principles here stated.

Now as for magnitude: In order to be beautiful, a living creature or anything else made up of parts not only must have its parts organized but must also have just the size that properly belongs to it. Beauty depends on size and order; hence an extremely minute creature could not be beautiful, for our vision becomes blurred as it approaches the point of imperceptibility, nor could an utterly huge creature be beautiful, for, unable to take it in all at once, the viewer finds that its unity and wholeness have escaped his field of vision—if, for example, it were an animal a thousand miles long.[1] Therefore, just as organized bodies and animals, if they are to be beautiful, must have size and such size as to be easily taken in by the eye, so plot, for the same reason, must have length and such length as to be easily held in the memory. The limit of length considered in relation to the public contests and production in sensible form has nothing to do with the art of poetry—if a hundred tragedies had to be presented in the contest, the performance would be timed by water clocks, as was actually done at one time, they say.[2] But considered in relation to the very nature of the thing itself, the limit is this: Invariably, the larger the plot is, while still remaining perspicuous, the more beautiful it is in virtue of its magnitude. Or, to express it in a simple formulation: If the length is sufficient to permit a change from bad fortune to good or from good fortune to bad to come about in an inevitable or probable sequence of events, this is a satisfactory limit of magnitude.[3]

1451a

8. The Plot: Further Remarks on Unity

Contrary to what some people think, a plot is not ipso facto a unity if it revolves about one man. Many things, indeed an endless number of things, happen to any one man some of which do not go together to form a unity, and similarly among the actions one man performs there are many that do not go together to produce a single unified action. Those poets seem all to have erred, therefore, who have composed a *Heracleid*, a *Theseid*, and other such poems, it being their idea evidently that since Heracles was one man, their plot was bound to be unified. But Homer, just as he excels in every other respect, seems in this matter also, either by art or natural instinct, to have taken the right view. In composing his *Odyssey*, he did not put into it every event that had befallen Odysseus—his being wounded on Mount Parnassus, for example, and his feigning madness when the host was assembling, neither of which events was at all a necessary or probable consequence of the other—but instead he constructed the *Odyssey* around a single action such as I am describing, and he did the same with the *Iliad*.[1] Consequently, just as in the other mimetic arts an imitation is unified when it is the imitation of a unified object,[2] so in poetry the plot, since it is the imitation of an action, must be the imitation of a unified action comprising a whole; and the events which are the parts of the plot must be so organized that if any one of them is displaced or taken away, the whole will be shaken and put out of joint;[3] for if the presence or absence of a thing makes no discernible difference, that thing is not part of the whole.

9. Poetry Represents the Universal in the Particular

From what has already been said, it will be evident that the poet's function is not to report things that have happened, but rather to tell of such things as might happen, things that are possibilities by virtue of being in themselves inevitable or probable. Thus the difference between the historian and the poet is not that the historian employs prose and the poet verse—the work of Herodotus could be put into verse, and it would be no less a history with verses than without them; rather the difference is that the one tells of things that have been and the other of such things as might be. Poetry, therefore, is a more philosophical and a higher thing than history, in that poetry tends rather to express the universal, history rather the particular fact.[1] A universal is: The sort of thing that (in the circumstances) a certain kind of person will say or do either probably or necessarily, which in fact is the universal that poetry aims for (with the addition of names for the persons); a particular, on the other hand is: What Alcibiades did or had done to him.[2] This [generalizing tendency] has now come out clearly in the case of comedy, where the poets, having constructed their plots out of probable incidents, then supply any names that may occur to them, and do not, like the iambic poets, take a particular individual as their subject.[3] In tragedy, however, the historical names are retained. Basically this is because possibility means credibility; until something happens we remain uncertain of its possibility, but what has happened obviously is possible, since if impossible, it would not have happened. Yet as a matter of fact there are some tragedies in which only one or two of the well-known names occur, the rest being invented, and other tragedies again in which there are no famous names at all. An example is Agathon's *Antheus*.[4] In this play, plot and names alike are invented, and yet it gives no less pleasure on that account. So there certainly is no need to make a point of adhering to the traditional stories on which tragedies are based. Indeed, it would be absurd to do so, since the

1451^b

well-known tales are well known only to a few, and nevertheless they give pleasure to all.

It is clear, then, from the foregoing remarks that the poet should be a maker[5] of plots more than a maker of verses, in that he is a poet by virtue of his imitation and he imitates actions. So even if on occasion he takes real events as the subject of a poem, he is none the less a poet, since nothing prevents some of the things that have actually happened from being of the sort that might probably or possibly happen, and it is in accordance with this that he is their poet.[6]

Among plots and actions of the simple type, the episodic form is the worst.[7] I call episodic a plot in which the episodes follow one another in no probable or inevitable sequence. Plots of this kind are constructed by bad poets on their own account, and by good poets on account of the actors; since they are composing entries for a competitive exhibition, they stretch the plot beyond what it can bear and are often compelled, therefore, to dislocate the natural order.[8] And it is not only an action complete in itself that tragedy represents; it also represents incidents involving pity and fear, and such incidents are most effective when they come unexpectedly and yet occur in a causal sequence in which one thing leads to another. For occurring in this way, they will have more of the marvelous about them than if they came to pass of themselves and by accident. (Indeed, things that actually do happen by accident seem most marvelous when they appear to be intentional, as when at Argos the statue of Mitys killed the man who had caused Mitys' death by falling down on him as he stood looking at it.[9] It is hard to believe that such things happen without design.) Plots of this kind, therefore, are necessarily better than others.

1452[a]

10. Simple and Complex Plots

Some plots are simple, others complex; indeed the actions of which the plots are imitation are at once so differentiated to begin with. Assuming the action to be continuous and unified, as already defined,[1] I call that action simple in which the change of fortune takes place without a reversal or recognition, and that action complex in which the change of fortune involves a recognition or a reversal or both.[2] These events [recognitions and reversals] ought to be so rooted in the very structure of the plot that they follow from the preceding events as their inevitable or probable outcome; for there is a vast difference between following from and merely following after.

11. Parts of the Plot: Reversal, Recognition, Suffering

Reversal (Peripety) is, as aforesaid, a change from one state of affairs to its exact opposite, and this, too, as I say, should be in conformance with probability or necessity.[1] For example, in *Oedipus*, the messenger comes to cheer Oedipus by relieving him of fear with regard to his mother, but by revealing his true identity, does just the opposite of this.[2] In *Lynceus* again, Lynceus is brought on expecting to die and Danaüs follows intending to put him to death, but as a result of what has gone before, it turns out that Danaüs is put to death and Lynceus is saved.[3]

Recognition, as the word itself indicates, is a change from ignorance to knowledge, leading either to friendship or to hostility on the part of those persons who are marked for good fortune or bad.[4] The best form of recognition is that which is accompanied by a reversal, as in the example from *Oedipus*. There are, to be sure, other forms of recognition—and, indeed, what I have just said may occur in reference to inanimate objects or anything whatever, and it is possible to discover that someone has or has not done something—but the form that has most to do with the plot, and most to do with the action, is the one I have mentioned; for a recognition joined thus with a reversal will be fraught with pity or with fear (the type of action tragedy is presumed to imitate) because misery and happiness alike will come to be realized in recognitions of this kind. Now since recognition involves more than one person, there are cases in which one of two persons already knows the other and the recognition is on one side only, and other cases in which recognition has to take place on both sides. Iphigeneia, for example, was recognized by Orestes from the sending of her letter, but a second recognition was required to reveal his identity to her.[5]

Two elements of the tragic plot, then, are Reversal and Recognition. A third element is Suffering *(pathos)*. We have said what reversal and recognition are; Suffering is an action of a destructive or painful description, such as the deaths that take place in the open [and not behind the scenes], agonies of pain, wounds, and so on.[6]

1452[b]

12. The Quantitative Parts of Tragedy[1]

Earlier I spoke of the parts of tragedy that are to be employed as formative elements. The following are the parts or separate sections into which it is divided quantitatively: Prologue, Episode, Exode, and

Choral part, this last again being divided into Parodos and Stasimon, which are found in all tragedies, and songs from the stage[2] and Kommoi, found only in some. The Prologue is the whole section preceding the entrance song (Parodos) of the chorus; an Episode a whole section between two complete choral odes; and the Exode the whole section after which there is no choral ode. In the choral part, the Parodos is the first continuous utterance of the chorus; a Stasimon is a choral ode without anapaestic and trochaic lines;[3] a Kommos is a lament in which chorus and actors both take part. Earlier I spoke of the parts of tragedy that are to be employed as formative elements; these are the parts or separate sections into which it is divided quantitatively.

13. The Best Form of Tragedy

Next in order after the points I have just dealt with,[1] it would seem necessary to specify what one should aim at and what avoid in the construction of plots, and what it is that will produce the effect proper to tragedy.

Now since in the finest kind of tragedy the structure should be complex and not simple, and since it should also be a representation of terrible and piteous events (that being the special mark of this type of imitation), in the first place, it is evident that good men ought not to be shown passing from prosperity to misfortune, for this does not inspire either pity or fear, but only revulsion; nor evil men rising from ill fortune to prosperity, for this is the most untragic plot of all—it lacks every requirement, in that it neither elicits human sympathy[2] nor stirs pity or fear. And again, neither should an extremely wicked man be seen falling from prosperity into misfortune, for a plot so constructed might indeed call forth human sympathy, but would not excite pity or fear, since the first is felt for a person whose misfortune is undeserved and the second for someone like ourselves—pity for the man suffering undeservedly, fear for the man like ourselves—and hence neither pity nor fear would be aroused in this case.[3] We are left with the man whose place is between these extremes. Such is the man who on the one hand is not pre-eminent in virtue and justice, and yet on the other hand does not fall into misfortune through vice or depravity, but falls because of some mistake;[4] one among the number of the highly renowned and prosperous, such as Oedipus and Thyestes and other famous men from families like theirs.

1453ª

It follows that the plot which achieves excellence will necessarily be single in outcome and not, as some contend, double, and will consist in a change of fortune, not from misfortune to prosperity, but the opposite, from prosperity to misfortune, occasioned not by depravity, but by some great mistake on the part of one who is either such as I have described or better than this rather than worse. (What actually has taken place confirms this; for though at first the poets accepted whatever myths came to hand, today the finest tragedies are founded upon the stories of only a few houses, being concerned, for example, with Alcmeon, Oedipus, Orestes, Meleager, Thyestes, Telephus, and such others as have chanced to suffer terrible things or to do them.) So, then, tragedy having this construction is the finest kind of tragedy from an artistic point of view. And consequently, those persons fall into the same error[5] who bring it as a charge against Euripides that this is what he does in his tragedies and that most of his plays have unhappy endings. For this is in fact the right procedure, as I have said; and the best proof is that on the stage and in the dramatic contests, plays of this kind seem the most tragic, provided they are successfully worked out, and Euripides, even if in everything else his management is faulty, seems at any rate the most tragic of the poets.

Second to this is the kind of plot that some persons place first, that which like the *Odyssey* has a double structure and ends in opposite ways for the better characters and the worse. If it seems to be first, that is attributable to the weakness of the audience, since the poets only follow their lead and compose the kind of plays the spectators want. The pleasure it gives, however, is not that which comes from tragedy, but is rather the pleasure proper to comedy; for in comedy those who in the legend are the worst of enemies—Orestes and Aegisthus, for example—end by leaving the scene as friends, and nobody is killed by anybody.

14. How to Arouse Pity and Fear

1453ᵇ   The effect of fear and pity may be created by spectacle; but it may also be created by the very structure of the events, and this method has priority and is the way of a better poet. For the plot should be so constructed that even without seeing the play, anyone who merely hears the events unfold will shudder and feel pity as a result of what is happening—which is precisely what one would experience in listening to the plot of *Oedipus*. To procure this effect by means of spectacle is less artistic in that it calls for external apparatus,[1] while those who produce through spectacle something that is not terrifying but only portentous in effect have no part in tragedy at all, for not every sort of pleasure is to be sought from tragedy, but only that which properly belongs to it.[2] And since the pleasure the poet is to provide is that

which comes from pity and fear through an imitation, clearly this
effect must be embodied in the events of the plot.

Let us consider, therefore, the kinds of occurrences that seem terrible or pitiful. Actions of this sort must, of course, happen between
persons who are either friends to one another or enemies or neither.
Now if enemy harms enemy, there is nothing to excite pity either in his
doing the deed or in his being on the point of doing it—nothing, that
is, but the actual suffering; and the same is true if the parties are
neither friends nor enemies. When, however, the tragic event occurs
within the sphere of the natural affections—when, for instance, a
brother kills or is on the point of killing his brother, or a son his father,
or a mother her son, or a son his mother, or something equally drastic is
done—that is the kind of event a poet must try for. There is, of course,
no possibility of altering the traditional stories—I mean Clytemnestra
being murdered by Orestes and Eriphyle by Alcmeon—but it is the
poet's duty to find a way of using even these traditional subjects well.

Let me say more clearly what I mean by using them well. It is
possible to have the action occur with full knowledge and awareness on
the part of those involved, as the early poets used to do and as Euripides does when he has Medea kill her children. It is possible also to do
the awful thing, but to do it in ignorance and then discover the relationship of the victim later, as Sophocles' Oedipus does. In this case, to
be sure, the deed is done outside the play, but it is done in the tragedy
itself, for example, by the Alcmeon of Astydamas and by Telegonus in
Odysseus Wounded.[3] A third possibility is for one who is about to do
one of these atrocious deeds in ignorance to discover the relationship
before he does it. There are no other possibilities, for the deed has
either to be done or not done and with knowledge or without knowledge.[4] Of these situations, the worst is for someone to be on the point
of doing the deed with knowledge, and then not do it. This is revolting
in itself, and is not tragic, since no suffering is involved. It is not
employed, therefore, by the poets except occasionally, as when Hae-   1454ᵃ
mon in *Antigone* fails to kill Creon.[5] The doing of the deed comes next
in order. The better way is for it to be done in ignorance, with the
recognition following afterward; there is then nothing revolting in the
act, and the recognition astounds us. The best situation, however, is
the last mentioned. It is exemplified in *Chresphontes,*[6] where Merope
is on the point of murdering her son, when she recognizes him and
desists, and in *Iphigeneia,* where the sister is about to slay her brother;
and in *Helle,*[7] where the son is about to give his mother up to the
enemy when he learns who she is.[8]

These considerations account for the fact mentioned earlier, that
not many families provide subjects for tragedies.[9] The poets, that is, in

seeking out tragic situations, discovered more by luck than lore how to contrive in their plots the kind of situation we have described. And this obliges them to keep returning for subjects to those few houses that have had such dire events befall them.

Enough, then, has now been said about the construction of the events and what the plots should be like in tragedy; [and hence we turn next to Character].

15. The Characters of Tragedy

With regard to the Characters there are four things to aim at. First and foremost is that the characters be good. The personages will have character if, as aforesaid, they reveal in speech or in action what their moral choices are, and a good character will be one whose choices are good. It is possible to portray goodness in every class of persons; a woman may be good and a slave may be good, though perhaps as a class women are inferior and slaves utterly base. The second requisite is to make the character appropriate. Thus it is possible to portray any character as manly, but inappropriate for a female character to be manly or formidable in the way I mean.[1] Third is to make the characters lifelike, which is something different from making them good and appropriate, as described above.[2] Fourth is to make them consistent. Even if the person being imitated is inconsistent and this is what the character is supposed to be, he should nevertheless be portrayed as consistently inconsistent.

There is an example of unnecessary baseness in the character of Menelaus in *Orestes*;[3] of the unsuitable and inappropriate in the lamentation of Odysseus in *Scylla* and in the declamation of Melanippe;[4] and of inconsistency in *Iphigeneia in Aulis*, where the Iphigeneia who begs to be spared bears no resemblance to the Iphigeneia who appears thereafter.[5]

In the characters and the plot construction alike, one must strive for that which is either necessary or probable, so that whatever a character of any kind says or does may be the sort of thing such a character will inevitably or probably say or do and the events of the plot may follow one after another either inevitably or with probability. (Obviously, then, the denouement of the plot should arise from the plot itself and not be brought about "from the machine," as it is in *Medea* and in the embarkation scene in the *Iliad*.[6] The machine is to be used for matters lying outside the drama, either antecedents of the action which a human being cannot know, or things subsequent to the action that have to be prophesied and announced; for we accept it that the gods see everything. Within the events of the plot itself, however, there should be nothing unreasonable, or if there is, it should be kept outside the play proper, as is done in the *Oedipus* of Sophocles.[7])

Inasmuch as tragedy is an imitation of persons who are better than the average, the example of good portrait painters should be followed. These, while reproducing the distinctive appearance of their subjects in a recognizable likeness, make them handsomer in the picture than they are in reality. Similarly, the poet when he comes to imitate men who are irascible or easygoing or have other defects of character should depict them as such and yet as good men at the same time. An example involving harshness is the way Agathon and Homer portray Achilles.[8]

These, then, are matters to be carefully observed, as also are matters appertaining to the sense perceptions that the poet's art necessarily entails, for in respect to these, too, it is often possible to miss the mark. A sufficient account of them has been given in my published discourse.[9]

16. Different Kinds of Recognition (*Anagnorisis*)

What Recognition is in general has already been explained.[1] To turn now to its several species, first (1) there is the form that is least artistic and, from poverty of invention, the one they use most—that is, recognition by marks or tokens. Such marks are sometimes congenital, as "the lance the earth-born bear," or the "stars" in Carcinus' *Thyestes*,[2] and sometimes acquired, either something on the person, like a scar, or external tokens such as necklaces or the boat in *Tyro*.[3] Even these, however, can be used in better or worse ways. Thus Odysseus is recognized by means of his scar in one way by the nurse and in another way by the swineherds.[4] The recognitions by the herdsmen, and all such recognitions as use tokens as proofs of identity, are artistically worse, while those that occur spontaneously like the one in the Bath Scene are better. Second (2) are recognitions obviously managed by the poet and inartistic for that reason. An instance is the way Orestes in *Iphigeneia* gets himself recognized as Orestes: Iphigeneia is spontaneously recognized through the letter, but Orestes speaks for himself in terms imposed by the poet and not by the plot.[5] The fault here is close to the one just mentioned, since he might just as well have had a few marks or tokens on him. Another example is the "voice of the shuttle" in Sophocles' *Tereus*.[6] A third type of recognition (3) is that which comes about through memory—i.e., a person's reaction upon seeing something. Thus in Dicaeogenes' *Cyprians*, the hero bursts into tears upon seeing the picture,[7] and in the Alcinous episode Odysseus, when he hears the minstrel, is reminded of the past and weeps;[8] therewith in both

1455ᵃ

cases they are recognized. Fourth (4) is recognition through reasoning. This is exemplified in the *Choephori:*[9] "Someone resembling me has come; no one but Orestes resembles me; therefore Orestes has come." Another example is the recognition suggested for *Iphigeneia* by Polyidus the Sophist.[10] It would be natural, he said, for Orestes to reflect that his sister had been sacrificed and here he was himself about to be sacrificed in turn. Again, in the *Tydeus* of Theodectes, the father says that he had come in search of his son only to meet with death himself.[11] In the *Phinidae,* the women upon seeing the place drew this conclusion about their fate: that here they were doomed to die, since this was the place where they had been exposed in infancy.[12] There is also (5) a composite kind of recognition resulting from faulty inference by one party or the other.[13] For instance, in *Odysseus the False Messenger,*[14] the point that Odysseus and no one else can string the bow is something set up by the poet and is the basic premiss, [and it remains so] even if the messenger did say that he would know the bow which he had not seen; but having him gain recognition by this second means [i. e., by identifying the bow] on the assumption that he was going to be recognized by the first means [stringing the bow] is a fallacy.[15]

Of all the forms of recognition, however, the best is that which springs from the events themselves, the shock of surprise having thus a probable basis. Such are the recognitions in the *Oedipus* of Sophocles and in *Iphigeneia:* it is probable that Iphigeneia should wish to send a letter. Only recognitions of this kind escape the artificiality of tokens and necklaces. Next best are recognitions that result from reasoning.

17. Practical Hints for Playwrights

The poet, as he constructs his plots and is working them out complete with language, should as far as possible place the action before his eyes; for in this way, seeing the events with the utmost vividness, as if they were taking place in his very presence, he will discern what is appropriate and will be least likely to overlook discrepancies. Witness to this point is the mistake that brought censure upon Carcinus. Amphiaraus came back from the sanctuary. This was not noticed if one did not visualize the action, but on the stage the play collapsed when the audience would not tolerate the oversight.[1] Also the poet should as far as possible work out the play with the appropriate dramatic gestures;[2] for among poets of equal ability, those who themselves are in the emotional states they depict are the most convincing; that is, one who is in the throes of distress conveys distress and one who is in a rage conveys anger most truthfully and accurately. For this reason, poetry is the art of a man of genius or of one having a touch of madness—the first sort are versatile, the second excitable.[3]

Whether one is using a traditional story or an invented story and composing it oneself, one should first set it down in a general outline, and only then proceed to expand it by fashioning the episodes. What I mean by taking this general view of the whole may be illustrated from *Iphigeneia*, thus: 1455b

> A certain young girl who had been offered in sacrifice vanished mysteriously from the sight of the sacrificers, and having been set down in another country where it was the custom to sacrifice foreigners to the goddess, became the priestess of this rite. Some time later it happened that the priestess's brother arrived. (The fact that he went there because the oracle for a certain reason[4] commanded it, and what he went for, are matters external to the plot.) Upon his arrival, he was seized and was on the point of being sacrificed when he revealed who he was (either in Euripides' way of managing it, or in that of Polyidus with the quite natural remark that evidently not only his sister but he also had to be sacrificed); and thereby his life was saved.

This done, it is now time to put in the characters' names[5] and to fashion the episodes, taking care to see that the episodes are appropriate, as are, for example, in *Orestes*[6] the fit of madness that leads to Orestes' capture and the ritual cleansing that leads to the escape. Note that in drama the episodes are short, whereas in epic poetry episodes are used to give the poem length. Thus the argument of the Odyssey is not long:

> A certain man has been absent from home for many years; he is kept under hostile surveillance by Poseidon; and he is alone. Besides, the situation at home is that suitors are dissipating his property and plotting against his son. But after suffering from storms at sea, the man returns, reveals himself to certain persons, and attacking his enemies comes off safe himself and destroys them.

This is the essential story; and all the rest consists of episodes.

18. Miscellaneous Observations

1. Complication and denouement. In every tragedy there is first the Complication and then the Denouement. The complication comprises the events outside the play itself and often also some of the events within the play, and the remainder is the denouement. I mean that the complication extends from the beginning up to the last moment before the change to good or bad fortune occurs, and that the denouement begins with that change and extends to the end of the play. For example, in the *Lynceus* of Theodectes, the complication includes the antecedent events and, within the play, the seizure of the child and that in turn of [the parents]; the denouement extends from the indictment for murder to the end.[1]

2. *Four kinds of tragedy.* There are four types of tragedy, corresponding in number to the "parts" already mentioned.[2] There is complex tragedy, the whole of which consists of reversal and recognition; tragedy of passion—for example, the various plays entitled *Ajax* or *Ixion;*[3] tragedy of character, such as the *Women of Phthia* and *Peleus;*[4] and fourth ***, such as the *Daughters of Phorcys* and *Prometheus* and all plays the scene of which is in Hades.[5] One should by all means endeavor to have all these types at his command, or at least most of them and the most important—especially in view of the way they harass the poets nowadays; good poets having existed in each case in the past, they now expect the single poet to surpass each one of these in his point of excellence.[6]

3. *How best to judge plays.* The right way to compare tragedy with tragedy is to consider no feature so much as the plot—that is, in plays having the same complication and denouement.[7] Many poets do well with the complication, only to fail with the denouement, but the one capacity should be brought into line with the other.

4. *Epic and dramatic plots.* One must bear in mind also what has been said repeatedly,[8] and not construct a tragedy on the plan of an epic poem (by epic I mean, having a multiplicity of stories)—as if, for example, someone were to dramatize the story of the *Iliad* in its entirety. In the epic, thanks to the length of the poem, the parts all assume their due proportions, but in plays the result of such a multiplicity is far from what was expected. One has only to note that those who have dramatized the *Sack of Troy* entire, instead of taking one part at a time as Euripides did, or the whole Niobe story instead of doing as Aeschylus did, invariably either have their plays hissed off or make but a poor showing in the competition.[9] In fact, the one occasion when even Agathon was driven from the stage was when he did this.

5. *The poet's steady aim.* It is remarkable how both in peripeties [i.e., complex plots] and in simple plots the poets keep their aim fixed on the effects they wish to produce—the tragic effect, that is, and the effect of human sympathy. The latter is our feeling when a clever but villainous man is outwitted, Sisyphus for example, or when a brave but

1456ᵃ

unjust man is defeated. This even has a kind of probability, if only in the sense of Agathon's comment, for it is probable that many improbable things will happen.[10]

6. *The chorus in tragedy.* The chorus ought to be regarded as one of the actors, and as being part of the whole and integrated into performance, not in Euripides' way but in that of Sophocles.[11] In the other poets,[12] the choral songs have no more relevance to the plot than if they belonged to some other play. And so nowadays, following the practice introduced by Agathon, the chorus merely sings interludes. But what difference is there between the singing of interludes and taking a speech or even an entire episode from one play and inserting it into another?

19. Thought and Language

Now that the other elements have been discussed, it remains to speak of Language and Thought.[1] As for Thought, this subject may best find its place in my discussion of rhetoric, since it belongs more properly to that field of study.[2] Under Thought come all the effects that are to be obtained through speech, and these fall under the heads of proving and refuting, stirring up emotions (pity, fear, anger, and the rest), and enlarging or belittling the importance of things. Obviously, in their actions as well as in their utterances, the personages will employ Thought in these same categories whenever they have to inspire pity or terror or convey a sense of importance or plausibility simply by what they do; the only difference being that the acts must make their impression immediately without verbal explanation, while the effects of the speech must be procured by the speaker and be the result of what he says, for if the intended impression were to be made independently of the speech and not by means of it, what need would there be for the speaker?[3]

To come to Language, one technical study relating to it concerns the Forms of Expression, knowledge of which properly belongs to the art of Elocution and to the specialist in that sort of thing—what is a command, what is a prayer, a statement, a question, an answer, and the like.[4] A poet's knowledge or ignorance of these matters is not a point on which criticism of any consequence is directed against his art. For what error would anyone suppose there to be in the words "Sing, goddess, the wrath,"[5] which Protagoras,[6] however, criticizes on the grounds that Homer thinks he is uttering a prayer when he is really giving an order. According to Protagoras, to bid someone do or not do

1456b

something is a command. Let us, therefore, leave this technicality aside as belonging to some other art and not to the art of poetry.

20. Language in General: Definitions[1]

Language, taken as a whole, is divisible into the following parts: the single letter, the syllable, the connective particle, the article[?], the noun, the verb, the inflection, the unified uterance.[2]

A letter is an indivisible sound—not every such sound, however, but one capable of uniting with others in a complex sound; the lower animals utter indivisible sounds, but not what I call a letter. These primary sounds are divided into vowels, semivowels, and mutes. A vowel is a letter having audible sound without the application [of the tongue or lips]; a semivowel is one having audible sound with such application—e.g., S and R; a mute—e.g., G and D—is one which, though made by application [of these organs], has no sound by itself but becomes audible when combined with letters having a sound. The letters owe their variety to their being produced by different conformations of the mouth or the different parts of it, to their being aspirated or not aspirated, to their being long or short, and, finally, to their being uttered with acute, grave, or intermediate tones. Detailed study of these matters belongs to the subject of metrics.[3]

A syllable is a nonsignificant sound composed of a mute and a letter having sound [vowel or semivowel]; for GR without A is a syllable as well as GRA. But differences of syllables is also a subject for metrics.

1457[a]   The Connective Particle[4] is (a) a nonsignificant sound—e.g. *men*, *êtoi*, *de*—which neither prevents nor causes formation of one significant sound [expression] out of two or more others, and which cannot correctly stand by itself at the beginning of a phrase; or (b) it is a nonsignificant sound, such as *amphi, peri*, etc., which functions to make one significant sound [expression] out of two or more significant sounds.

An Article[?] is a nonsignificant sound which marks the beginning or end or a division [of an expression].

A Noun[5] is a composite significant sound, not indicating time, no part of the composite being by itself significant; for even when a noun is composed of two others we do not treat these as separately significant; e.g., in the name Theodore -*dore* ["gift"] is not significant.

A Verb is a composite significant sound, indicating time, no part of the composite being by itself significant, just as in nouns. Thus "men" or "white" gives no indication of "when," but "walks" and "has walked" add to their meaning the indication respectively of present and past time.

Inflection applies to nouns or verbs, as when the meaning is "of" or "to" something, and so forth; or when the reference is to one or more than one, as "man" and "men"; or again it may be a mode of utterance, for example, a question or a command: "walked?" and "Walk!" being inflections of the verb in these two forms of utterance.[6]

A unified utterance is a composite significant sound, some parts of which have independent meaning. Not every such utterance is a combination of nouns and verbs; it can exist without verbs, as, for example, the definition of man.[7] However, it will always include a member having independent meaning, as "Cleon" in "Cleon walks."[8] The unified utterance is a unit in either of two ways, either because what it signifies is itself a unit or because it is a combination of several parts. Thus the *Iliad* is unified by combination, the definition of man by signifying one thing.

21. Language in General: Classification of Words

Words are of two kinds, simple words—those like *gê* (earth) that are not compounds of significant parts—and double words.[1] The latter are compounds consisting either of a significant and a nonsignificant part (though in the compound these are not recognized as significant or nonsignificant), or of two parts both of which have meaning.[2] There may also be triple and quadruple words and indeed multiple words, as, for example, most of the names of the people of Marseilles [? in a mock heroic poem]—Hermocaicoxanthus.[3]

1457[b]

Every word is either (1) the ordinary current word, or (2) a foreign word, or (3) a metaphor, or (4) an ornamental word, or (5) a coined word, or a word (6) lengthened or (7) curtailed or (8) otherwise altered in form.

By "current word" I mean a word used by everyone [in any particular region], and by "foreign word" a word used by others elsewhere. Obviously, the same word may be both current and foreign, but not for the same people; *sigynon* (lance) is a current word in Cyprus but a foreign word for us.[4]

Metaphor is the application to one thing of the name belonging to another. We may apply (a) the name of a genus to one of its species, or (b) the name of a species to its genus, or (c) the name of one species to another of the same genus, or (d) the transfer may be based on a proportion. Examples:

(a) From genus to species: "Here stands my ship,"[5] since *to be at anchor* is a special form of *standing still.*

(b) From species to genus: "Truly *ten thous*and noble deeds hath Odysseus done,"[6] for *ten thousand* is a large number and is here used in place of the generic *many.*

(c) From species to species: "*drawing* off the life with bronze" and "*cutting* off [streams of water?] with unwearied bronze [vessels?]," where "drawing off" is put for "cutting off" and "cutting off" for "drawing off," both expressions being species of the genus "take away."[7]

(d) The meaning of metaphor ,by analogy [or proportional metaphor] is that when among four things the second is related to the first as the fourth is related to the third, one may substitute the fourth for the second or the second for the fourth.[8] And sometimes the term related to the proper term in the analogy is added to the metaphor, thus: The wine cup is to Dionysus as the shield is to Ares, and therefore one may call a wine cup "the shield of Dionysus" and the shield "the wine cup of Ares."[9] Again, old age is to life what evening is to day; and one may speak of evening as "the old age of the day" (either thus or as Empedocles puts it)[10] and of old age as "the evening of life" or "the sunset of life." In some cases there are terms of the proportion for which actually we have no word but which nevertheless will find expression in metaphor. Thus to cast seed is to sow, but there is no special word for the casting of its rays by the sun; this, however, is to sunlight what sowing is to seed, and hence the expression: "sowing a god-created flame."[11] There is still another way in which this type of metaphor may be used. Having called one thing by the name of another, we can deny it some special attribute of this thing—as one might call a shield not the wine cup "of Ares," but the "wineless" wine cup.[12]

A coined word is a word not used at all by any group of speakers but simply invented by the poet; for apparently there are some words of this kind, as *ernygas* ("sprouters"?) for *kerata* ("horns") and *arêtêr* ("supplicator") for *hiereus* ("priest").[13]

An Expanded Word is one in which a vowel that is usually short is treated as long, or one in which an extra syllable has been inserted. A Curtailed Word is one from which some part has been taken away. Examples of expanded words: *poleôs* for *poleôs*, *Pêlêïadeô* for *Pêleidou*; of curtailed words: krî (for *krithe*), dô (for *dôma*),[14] and *ops* (for *opsis*) in *mia ginetai amphoterôn ops.*[15] A word is Altered when part of the usual form is kept and part is refashioned. Example, *dexiteron kata mazon* for *dexion.*[16]

Nouns themselves are masculine or feminine, or else intermediate between these.[17] Masculine [and not feminine] are all that end in nu,

1458[a]

rho, or sigma or compounds of sigma (i.e., psi and ksi);[18] feminine are those ending in vowels that are always long (i.e., eta and omega) or in alpha among vowels that may be long or short. Thus the masculine and feminine terminations are equal in number, the compounds psi and ksi counting as sigma. No noun ends in a mute or in an invariably short vowel [epsilon or omicron]; only three end in iota, namely *meli* (honey), *kommi* (gum), and *peperi* (pepper); and five end in upsilon: <*pôu* (flock), *nâpu* (mustard), *gonu* (knee), *doru* (spear), *astu* (town)>.[19] The intermediates end in these vowels and in nu and sigma.[20]

22. The Language of Poetry

Of Diction[1] the prime virtue is to be clear without being commonplace. Diction is at its clearest when composed of words in everyday use, but then it is commonplace, as is exemplified by the poetry of Cleophon and Sthenelus.[2] On the other hand, an impressive diction, one that escapes the ordinary, results from the use of strange words, by which I mean foreign words, metaphors, expanded words, and whatever departs from normal usage. However, anything composed entirely in such language will either be a riddle or a barbarism—a riddle if composed in metaphors, a barbarism if in foreign words alone. In fact, the very idea of a riddle is to describe a given object by means of a string of absurdities, a thing that cannot of course be done by any combination of the proper terms, but can be done if you combine the corresponding metaphors, as in "I saw a man welding bronze on another man with fire,"[3] and similar riddles. In like manner, a combination of foreign words produces a barbarism.

What is needed, therefore, is a blend, so to speak, of these ingredients, since the unfamiliar element (the foreign word, the metaphor, the ornamental word, and the other types mentioned) will save the diction from being commonplace and drab, while the colloquial element will ensure its clarity. By no means least important in what they contribute at once to clarity and to unfamiliarity are the expanded, curtailed, and altered forms of words. These will provide the element of unfamiliarity insofar as deviation from the normal forms makes them unusual, while the fact that they are in part ordinary words will ensure clarity. Unwarranted, therefore, are the objections of those who censure this kind of expression and hold the poet[4] up to ridicule for using it, as for instance the elder Eucleides does. Making poetry is easy, he says, if they let you stretch out the words as much as you please, and therewith he produces some burlesque lines in the style in question:[5]

1458[b]

Ἐπιχάρην εἶδον Μαραθῶνάδε βαδίζοντα
Epicharên eidon Marathônade badizonta,

and

Οὐκ ἂν γ'ἐράμενος τὸν ἐκείνου ἐλλέβορον.
Ouk an g'eramenos [?] ton ekeinou elleboron.[6]

Agreed that too obvious a use of lengthened words becomes ridiculous, but moderation has its place in all the stylistic devices, and Eucleides might have achieved the same effect with metaphors, foreign words, and the rest, if he had treated them abusively with the express purpose of raising a laugh. Try substituting the normal words in a verse of epic poetry, and you will realize what a difference the lengthened forms make when handled properly. The same with foreign words, metaphors, and the other forms, anyone who replaced them with the regular words would see that what I say is right.

To illustrate: The same iambic line is found both in Aeschylus and in Euripides, but Euripides has altered just one word, putting a strange word in place of a common everyday one, and as a result his line seems fine and the other poor in comparison. Aeschylus in his *Philoctetes* has it thus:

φαγέδαινα ἥ μου σάρκας ἐσθίει ποδός,[7]
phagedaina hê mou sarkas esthiei podos

and what Euripides did was to change ἐσθίει ("eats") to θοινᾶται ("feasts on"). Again, in the line,

νῦν δέ μ' ἐὼν ὀλίγος τε καὶ οὐτιδανὸς καὶ ἀεικής,[8]
nun de m'eôn oligos te kai outidanos kai aeikês

suppose one were to substitute the ordinary words and say:

νῦν δέ μ' ἐὼν μικρός τε καὶ ἀσθενικὸς καὶ ἀειδής,[9]
nun de m'eôn mikros te kai asthenikos kai aeidês

and similarly in

δίφρον ἀεικέλιον καταθεὶς ὀλίγην τε τράπεζαν,[10]
diphron aeikelion katatheis oligên te trapezan

say:

δίφρον μοχθηροῦ καταθεὶς μικράν τε τράπεζαν.
diphron mochthêrou katatheis mikran te trapezan.

And suppose *êiones boôsin* (ἠιόνες βοόωσιν) ("the sea beaches bel-
low")[11] to be replaced by *êiones krazousin* (ἠιόνες κράζουσιν) ("the sea
beaches cry out"). Also, Ariphrades[12] made fun of the tragic poets for
using locutions that no one would employ in ordinary speech, such as
dômatôn apo (δωμάτων ἄπο) ("from the houses away") instead of
apo dômatôn (ἀπὸ δωμάτων) ("away from the houses") and *sethen*
(σέθεν) ("of thine") and *ego de nin* (ἐγὼ δέ νιν) [where *nin* (νιν) is
an archaic third-person pronoun] and *Achilleôs peri* (Ἀχιλλέως πέρι)
("Achilles about") for *peri Achilleôs* (περὶ Ἀχιλλέως) ("about Achil-   1459ᵃ
les"), and so on. But all such expressions, just because they are not in
the current vocabulary, give distinction to the poet's language; and
that is what Ariphrades failed to understand.

To give appropriate treatment to the kinds of words here discussed,
including compounds and foreign words, is in every case important, but
most important by far is to have an aptitude for metaphor. This alone
cannot be had from another but is a sign of natural endowment; since
being good at making metaphors is equivalent to being perceptive of
resemblances. And among these verbal forms, compounds are best fit-
ted for dithyrambs, foreign words for heroic verse, and metaphors for
iambic verse. In heroic verse all the forms may be used; but in iambic
verse, where the aim is to imitate the spoken language as closely as
possible, only those forms are appropriate which would also be used in
prose—that is, the current word, the metaphor, and the ornamental
word.[13]

Let us regard the foregoing as a sufficient account of tragedy and of
imitation in the mode of direct action.

23. Epic Poetry

But as for the imitative art that is narrative [in manner] and employs
metrical language [as its medium], it is evident that, just as in tragedies, its plots should be dramatic in structure—that is, should involve a
single action, whole and complete in itself, having a beginning, a middle, and an end, so that like one whole living creature it may produce
its appropriate pleasure—and that its structure should not resemble
histories, which necessarily present not a single action but a single

period of time with all that happened therein to one or more persons, no matter how little relation one event may have had with another.[1] (Thus though occurring at the same time,[2] the naval battle at Salamis and the battle with the Cathaginians in Sicily did not converge to a common end, and similarly in a time sequence there are cases in which one event follows another without uniting in a single issue.) Yet perhaps the majority of the poets do precisely that. Hence on this point also, Homer, as we have said of him before,[3] might seem divine compared with the others, in that, though the war had indeed a beginning and an end, even so he did not attempt to make the whole of it the subject of his poem, since he realized that if he did so, the narrative was going to be too vast to be easily embraced in one view, or if he limited its extent, the variety of incidents would make it too complicated. As it is, he has selected one part of the war as his theme and used many of the other parts as episodes, the Catalogue of Ships,[4] for example, and the other episodes with which he spaces out his poem. The others make their poems about one man, or about one period of time, or else about one action that has many parts, as is done by the authors of the *Cypria* and the *Little Iliad*.[5] And so, while the *Iliad* and the *Odyssey* each furnish the subject for but a single tragedy, or at most for two, the *Cypria* has furnished themes for many tragedies and the *Little Iliad* themes for more than eight—an *Award of the Arms*, a *Philoctetes*, a *Neoptolemus*, a *Eurypylus*, a *Beggary*, a *Laconian Women*, a *Sack of Troy*, a *Sailing of the Fleet*, a *Sinon*, and a *Trojan Women*.[6]

1459b

24. Epic Poetry (Continued)

Likewise, epic poetry should include the same types as tragedy[1]—the simple, the complex, the poem of character, and the poem of passion; and should have the same essential elements, except music and spectacle, since an epic poem needs reversals and recognitions and sufferings, and ought also to have a good quality of thought and language. All these things Homer was the first to use, and he used them fully; for his two poems are complementary in structure, the *Iliad* being simple in plot and a poem of passion, and the *Odyssey* complex (it has recognitions throughout) and a poem of character; moreover they surpass all other poems in excellence of language and thought.[2]

However, epic poetry differs from tragedy in the length of the composition and in meter. As to length, the formulation we have already made is valid[3]—that it should be possible to embrace the beginning and the end in one view. Such would be the case if the poems were shorter than the old epic poems and approached the length of the group of tragedies presented at a single hearing.[4] Yet relative to its extension in magnitude, epic poetry has a very distinct advantage in that in tragedy it is not possible to represent various parts [of the story] as being enacted simultaneously, but only the one that the players have in hand on the stage,[5] whereas in epic the narrative form makes it possible to describe many parts as completed within the same time, and through these, if they are appropriate, the bulk of the poem is enlarged.[6] This, accordingly, is an advantage that epic poetry has, making for grandeur and the diversion of the hearer through the introduction of episodes of dissimilar character; for uniformity soon palls and is a reason for failure in the case of tragedies.[7]

As for the meter, the heroic [hexameter] proved, as the result of trial, to be the fitting one. Indeed, it would seem out of keeping if anyone were to compose a narrative imitation in some other meter or in a combination of meters, since in comparison with the other verse forms the heroic [hexameter] is the most deliberate and weighty. (These qualities make it especially receptive of foreign words and metaphors—for in this respect[8] narrative imitation goes beyond the other kinds.) The iambic trimeter and the trochaic tetrameter, on the other hand, are verses of movement, the latter being proper to the dance and the former to [dramatic] action. To combine these meters, as Chaeremon does, would be still more out of place in epic. No one, therefore, has ever composed a long poem in any other meter than the heroic; but nature herself, as we have said, teaches us to choose the meter appropriate to it.[9]

1460[a]

In addition to the many other reasons why Homer deserves admiration, there is this in particular, that he alone among the epic poets has not failed to understand the part the poet himself should take in his poem. The poet should, in fact, speak as little as possible in his own person, since in what he himself says he is not an imitator. Now the other poets are themselves on the scene throughout their poems, and their moments of imitation are few and far between, but Homer, after a few introductory words, at once brings on a man or a woman or some other personage,[10] and not one of them characterless but each with a character of his own.

The marvelous is an element that should of course be embodied in tragedies, but that which is a prime source of the marvelous—namely, the irrational—can be more freely introduced in epic poetry where we do not have the performer of the act directly before our eyes; for the Pursuit of Hector would seem ridiculous if it took place on the stage—the army just standing by and taking no part in the chase and Achilles shaking his head at them[11]—but in the poem the absurdity goes unnoticed. And the marvelous is enjoyable; note how everyone in reporting a piece of news adds his own embellishments with the idea of pleasing the listener.

It is Homer especially who has taught the other poets how to tell lies as they should be told. This is done by the use of paralogism.[12] That is, when the existence of one thing entails the existence of a second thing, or one occurrence entails a second occurrence, people assume that if this second thing exists, the antecedent also exists or occurs; but this is not so. If, then, the antecedent is a lie, but there is something else that would necessarily exist or happen if it were the truth, one should add this thing to the lie, for knowing this second thing to be true, our mind wrongly infers that the antecedent is true also. The Bath Scene provides an example.[13]

What is impossible yet probable should be preferred to that which is possible but incredible; plots should never be constructed out of irrational parts.[14] Best that there should not be anything irrational in them at all, but if there is, let it be outside the story told, as, in *Oedipus Tyrannus*, Oedipus's not knowing how Laius died, and not something in the play, as their reporting of the Pythian Games in *Electra* or in the *Mysians* the man's having come all the way from Tegea to Mysia without uttering a word.[15] To argue that without the part in question the plot would be ruined is ridiculous; no such plots should be constructed in the first place. If, however, such a part has been included, and is made to appear relatively plausible, it may be accepted in spite of its absurdity; since, even in the *Odyssey*, the irrational features of the Landing Scene would in themselves not have been tolerable, as would be apparent if a bad poet were to handle them, but as it is, with the aid of the other good features, the poet obliterates these and mitigates the absurdity.[16]

The place for elaborate diction is in the less vital passages—that is, passages not intended to reveal either character or thought; for, the other way round, where character and thought are to be revealed, too brilliant a diction will obscure them.[17]

25. Critical Problems and Their Solutions[1]

Critical problems and their solutions fall into different classes, the number and nature of which will be made clear by the considerations that follow.

Basic assumptions. Since the poet is an imitator, exactly like a painter or any other maker of images, he must necessarily in every case be imitating one of three objects: things as they once were or now are; or things as people say or suppose they were or are; or things as they ought to be. The language in which these things are narrated will include foreign words and metaphors and various abnormalities of diction, for this is a license we grant to the poets. And further, correctness in politics is not the same thing as correctness in poetry, nor is correctness in any other art the same as in poetry, but in poetry itself error is of two kinds, that which involves the art itself and that which is incidental.[2] Thus the art itself is involved if one has decided to imitate <a certain object and fails to represent it correctly through>[3] incompetence; but it is a nonessential error if one decides by mistake to represent a horse with both right legs thrown forward,[4] or if the fault involves a particular art, medicine, for example, or any other art whatsoever.[5] So then, it is in the light of the foregoing postulates that one should examine the criticisms that fall within the general problems, and find the answers to them.

Criticisms relating to the art itself (i.e., Imitation). First, criticisms relating to the art itself:[6]

1. "The thing represented is impossible." That is indeed a fault, but it is justified if doing so achieves the artistic purpose—this has already been stated: if doing so makes this or some other part of the poem more exciting. An example is the Pursuit of Hector.[7] It is not justified, however, if the end could have been achieved equally well or better in strict conformity with the special art there relevant;[8] for, if possible, no mistakes should be made at all.

2. Also we should inquire whether the mistake involves the art itself or is incidental. Thus, the error is less if the artist did not know that female deer have no horns than if he failed to draw a recognizable picture.[9]

3. Again, if something is criticized as not being true to fact, the answer may be: Yes, but that is how it ought to be—just as Sophocles, too, said that he portrayed men as they ought to be, while Euripides portrayed them as they are.[10]

4. But if the representation is neither true to fact nor an idealization, the solution may be that it accords with what men say. So with what [the poets] tell about the gods; this is perhaps neither the better way of speaking about them, nor the truth; it may be [as reprehensible] as Xenophanes thought it was—still, it is what men say.[11]   1461ª

5. In other cases, perhaps not "better than mere fact" but "thus it once was" is the answer. So in the problem about the arms—"Their spears stood pointed upward, butts in the ground": that was the custom in those days—and still is the custom in Illyria.[12]

6. In dealing with the question whether that which has been said or done by someone is right or wrong, we must not only have regard to

the moral quality, good or bad, of the act or utterance in and for itself, but must consider who says or does it, to whom it is said or done, on what occasion, how, and from what motive—whether, for example, the purpose is to bring about a greater good or to avert a greater evil.

Criticisms relating to language. In meeting other criticisms, one should pay attention to the use of language.

7. The criticism may be met by applying the category "foreign word." Thus in οὐρῆας μὲν πρῶτον [the mules first of all], perhaps by οὐρῆας Homer does not mean "mules" but "sentinels."[13] And his description of Dolon, ὅς ῥ᾽ ἦ τοι εἶδος μὲν ἔην κακός [who indeed was ill favored in form], may mean, not misshapen in body, but having an ugly face, since in Crete "well formed" (εὐειδής) is the regular word for "fair-faced" (εὐπρόσωπος).[14] And "mix the drink" ζωρότερον may not mean to mix it "stronger," as for heavy drinkers, but "faster."[15]

8. Again, the expression may be explained as metaphorical. So in "Now all the gods and men slept throughout the night" followed presently by "whenever he [Agamemnon] looked toward the Trojan plain, [he was amazed at] the din of flutes and pipes," the word "all" is used metaphorically for "many," since "all" is a species of the genus "many."[16] And "alone without a share" is metaphorical, since the best-known instance is taken for the only one.[17]

9. The solution may lie in a change of accent. In this way, Hippias of Thasos solved the difficulty in δίδομεν δέ οἱ εὖχος ἀρέσθαι[18] and again in τὸ μὲν οὗ καταπύθεται ὄμβρῳ.[19]

10. In other cases, punctuation may provide the answer, as in Empedocles' sentence: "Suddenly things became mortal that before had learnt to be immortal and things unmixed before mixed."[20]

11. In others, we must take account of an ambiguity, as in "night is more than two thirds gone and a third remains," where "more than" is ambiguous, [since the word πλέω may also mean "fully"].[21]

12. In others again, we may appeal to a habitual mode of speech. As a mixture of wine and water is called simply "wine," so, analogously, the poet speaks of "a greave of newly wrought tin."[22] And on the same principle by which iron workers are always called "braziers," Ganymede is said to be "the wine pourer of Zeus," though gods do not drink wine.[23] But this might also be explained as metaphorical.

Right and wrong methods in criticism. Whenever a particular word involves an apparent contradiction, the thing to do is to consider all the possible meanings it may have in the passage in question. For example, in "there the brazen spear was stopped" we should consider all the possible meanings "to be checked there" admits of, trying it in this sense and that sense, for the best understanding of it.[24] This method of procedure is just the opposite of that which Glaucon[25] describes. Certain critics, he says, begin with an unlikely assumption about some point, then condemn the meaning they have themselves assumed and give reasons against it, and they censure the poet for having said what they imagine he has said, if this is in contradiction to what they and only they have thought. The question of Icarius has been treated in this way. They assume that Icarius was a Laconian; therefore it is an absurdity that Telemachus, on his visit to Lacedaemon, does not meet him there.[26] But perhaps it is rather as the Cephalonians say, for by their account it was in their country that Odysseus married and the name is not Icarius but Icadius; and hence very likely the problem arises from a [textual] error.[27]

Summation. In general, we should justify the Impossible by referring it to poetic effect, or to the principle of enhancement, or to received opinion. Thus in reference to poetic effect, a convincing impossibility is preferable to that which, though possible, is unconvincing;[28] and <in reference to enhancement, if it is impossible> that there should be men such as, for example, Zeuxis portrayed, then it may be a case of betterment—the ideal should surpass the reality. The Improbable [or Irrational] should be justified by "what men say," and also by the fact that sometimes the thing in question is not improbable—"it is probable that something improbable will happen."[29] In examining Contradictions we should proceed as one does when testing [possible fallacious] refutations in a debate—i.e., "whether the same thing and in relation to the same thing and in the same sense"[30]—applying these tests to the poet also [as well as to the debater] either in reference to the things he actually says or to what a reasonable person would suppose him to mean.[31] But censure on the grounds of Improbability or of Depravity is justified if the poet brings them in when there is no need for them at all, as Euripides' Aegeus is needlessly improbable[32] and his Menelaus in the *Orestes* needlessly base.[33]

Thus there are just five classes of problems from which critics draw their strictures, since whenever they object to something it is always because they find it either (1) Impossible, or (2) Improbable, or (3) Immoral, or (4) Contradictory, or (5) Incorrect as regards a special art. And we in turn must proceed from the same five classes of objections when we look for solutions. The solutions themselves are twelve in number.

26. Which Is Better—Epic Poetry or Tragedy?

Someone might raise the question whether the epic or the tragic form of imitation is better.[1] Thus: —if the less vulgar form is the better and that form which is addressed to the better audience is always the less vulgar, clearly the form that relies entirely on imitation is too vulgar by far; for convinced that the spectators never comprehend what is meant unless the actor adds something on his own, the players keep up a vast stir of activity and common flutists, for example, will go reeling about if they have to represent the throwing of a discus, or will clutch at the chorus leader if their music depicts Scylla.[2] Tragedy, then, is of such a character; it is like what the older generation of actors thought about those who came after them—Mynniscus used to call Callipides an ape for what he regarded as his extravagant style of acting, while much the same was said of Pindarus, and as these later

1462[a] actors stand in relation to the earlier ones, so the tragic art as a whole stands in relation to epic.[3] In short, epic poetry, they tell us, is addressed to a superior audience who have no need of gestures and postures, tragedy to the common crowd. Therefore, if tragedy is vulgar, obviously it will be inferior.[4]

Now in the first place, the complaint does not bear on the art of poetry, it bears on the art of acting, since it is also possible for a rhapsode to overdo the gesticulation when reciting epic poetry, as Sosistratus did, and for the singer in a singing contest to do so, as did Mnasitheus of Opus.[5] Then, too, not every form of bodily movement is to be condemned, unless we are to condemn the dance itself, but only the attitudes and gestures of ignoble persons—which is just the objection formerly made to Callipides and repeated nowadays about other actors, that their women are anything but ladies. And again, tragedy succeeds in producing its proper effect even without any movement at all, just as epic poetry does, since when it is merely read the tragic force is clearly manifested.[6] So then, if it is superior in all other respects, this at least is no necessary part of it.[7]

In the next place, [tragedy is in fact the better form] because (1) it has everything that epic poetry has (for it can even employ the epic meter),[8] and has in addition an element of no small importance in its music, which intensifies our pleasure in the highest degree;[9] then also (2) it has the advantage of vividness both when read and when acted;

1462[b] again (3) it excels because in tragedy the imitation fulfils its purpose in shorter compass—that which is more concentrated gives greater pleasure than that which is dispersed over a great length of time: I mean, for example, if someone were to lay out the *Oedipus* of Sophocles in the same number of lines as the *Iliad*; and again (4) the epic poets have a less unified type of imitation (witness the fact that any such poem supplies subjects for several tragedies), and consequently if ever they do make a poem of unified plot, either the tale will be concisely told and create a sense of abruptness, or it will conform to the normal epic length and seem watery; and I mean that the latter will be the case if the poem is put together out of a plurality of actions, as, for example, the *Iliad* has many such parts, and the *Odyssey* also, each part having a magnitude of its own; and yet these particular poems are as well constructed as an epic poem can be, and come as near as possible to being imitations of a single action. So, then, if tragedy is superior to epic poetry in all these respects, and excels it besides in [performing] the function for which the art exists (for these imitations should give us not just any pleasure but precisely the pleasure we have indicated), it is clear that tragedy is the better form of the two inasmuch as it succeeds better than the epic in achieving the end in view.[10]

Let this then be our account of Tragedy and Epic Poetry—their general nature; the number and variety of their species and constituent parts; the causes of success or failure; and critical problems with their solutions . . . [11]

Notes to the Translation

1. THE MIMETIC ARTS

1. On the scientific relevance of the opening statement, see Introduction, p. 9. The "primary elements" are the genus Imitation and the *differentiae*, which alone are the subject of Chapters 1–3 and are not there drawn up into definitions of the species. These might come later if needed; we actually get only a definition of tragedy (Chapter 6).

In its general nature (literally, "in itself"), the art of poetry is seen immediately below to be the art of imitation *(mimêsis)* in the medium of language. It exists, of course, only in its specific forms: epic poetry, tragedy, comedy, dithyramb, and nome. That imitation is a properly chosen genus is certain, since imitating is the common and essential feature of all these arts. Since what is imitated is primarily human actions, plot, the imitation of the action, is of first importance. In the *Poetics*, as it has come down to us, only tragedy and epic poetry are dealt with, the latter being treated as a form of tragedy; the discussion of comedy, if ever completed, is lost. The dithyramb and nome probably did not receive separate treatment. The characteristic effect or potentiality *(dynamis)* of tragedy is found to be its capacity to give "the pleasure . . . that . . . comes from pity and fear through an imitation" (Chapter 14), and presumably this is also the effect of epic poetry (Chapter 26). The "parts" of tragedy turn out to be six in number; Plot, Character, Thought, Language, Spectacle, and Music; but only the first four, coinciding with the "parts" of epic, directly concern the art of poetry .

The arts of imitation in language thus form a viable "field of study" *(methodos)*, and apparently Aristotle wishes to reserve for them alone the name of poetry. He denies the name of poet to Empedocles because Empedocles does not "imitate" (1447ª28); and since he dismisses the lyric parts of tragedy from the art of poetry, placing them with Music, we may perhaps infer that he would place all lyric poetry under the musical art. He is aware that in limiting poetry to *mimêsis* he goes against common Greek usage, for which all compositions in verse were poetry. In fact, in less scientific contexts Aristotle himself calls Empedocles and Alcaeus poets.

2. The dithyramb was an elaborate choral song with narrative content (myth) originally associated with the worship of Dionysus. The etymology of the word is unknown. In the course of the fifth century the dithyramb lost the strophic form of lyric and became more dramatic. Like tragedy and comedy, it was performed in poetical contests. At the City Dionysia in the fifth century there were presented ten dithyrambs, three tetralogics, each consisting of three tragedies and one satyr play, and from three to five comedies. This program was still followed in the fourth century, except that it became customary to give only one satyr

play at the beginning of the contest and to revive an old play outside the contest proper. No great reputations seem to have been made in the dithyramb after the middle of the fourth century. See A. Pickard-Cambridge, *The Dramatic Festivals of Athens*, rev. ed. by T. B. L. Webster (Oxford, 1953), p. 80.

3. I. e., the *aulos* and the *cithara*. It is convenient to retain the conventional translation of these words, although the *aulos* is thought to have been more like the clarinet or oboe than the flute, and the *cithara* was more elaborate than the lyre. They were the chief musical instruments for public performance, and their music, whether purely instrumental, or more commonly accompanied by words, was a highly sophisticated art, apparently mimetic in character in that it not only conveyed moods, but could suggest actions and was judged by its ethical qualities. The music of the *aulos* was felt to be strongly emotional and exciting, that of the *cithara* more sedate and noble. Both were used in drama. It is probably unnecessary to suppose that here and just below Aristotle is thinking of purely instrumental music; "most" of the music for *aulos* and *cithara* would have words, so far as we know, but the art of the aulist or citharist, as such, is without words.

4. Art in general is "a habit of production joined with correct reasoning" (*Nic. Eth.* 6.4, 1140ᵃ6-10)—e.g., the skilled production of a house or a bed. It always has a purpose. There is a kind of art that produces, not useful objects, but imitations of life and reality—e.g., painting, sculpture, and poetry—and its purpose is to give pleasure, since taking pleasure in imitations is a basic human instinct (Chapter 4). On the word "imitation" see the Introduction, pp. 8-9. Since imitation is essential, Aristotle sometimes prefers to speak of the poet's "imitation" instead of his "poem," and he generally uses the verb "to imitate" as meaning, not "to copy," but "to give an imitation"—e.g., "to given an imitation of men in action." In this meaning it is often convenient to translate it as "represent."

5. "In language alone . . . ," literally, "the art imitating only with bare words or the (bare) meters"—i.e., in either case words without melody, but in the latter case words having rhythm. The spoken or unsung forms of verse are the dactylic hexameter, the iambic trimeter, the trochaic tetrameter, and the elegiac distich (Else, p. 56).

6. Sophron and his son Xenarchus were Syracusans of the late fifth century B.C. Their mimes or short prose dialogues presented characteristic moments of daily life and probably furnished models for the dialogues featuring Socrates, first written, according to Aristotle (frg. 72), by Alexamenus of Teos. The (to us) conspicuous absence of Plato's name here is in accord with the impersonal character of the *Poetics*.

7. There would be no name embracing mimes and dialogues even if these were written in verse because in verse, too, there is no name that distinguishes verbal imitations as such, the vulgar nomenclature being based entirely on types of meter.

8. Empedocles of Acragas in Sicily (ca. 493-433 B.C.) composed his work *On Nature* and his *Purifications* in hexameters. He is here honorably distinguished from Homer, and in the dialogue *On Poets*, Aristotle (frg. 70) expressed a just

admiration of his metaphorical style and called him "Homeric." But in the *Rhetoric* (3, 1407ᵃ35) he thinks he wrote in verse and in his style in order to dazzle his readers and conceal his poverty of thought. Since Homer was "the poet" *par excellence,* Aristotle is not far out of line in his apparent wish to limit this word to the makers of imitations in verse; he would hardly venture to call Sophron and Xenarchus poets.

9. Chaeremon, a contemporary of Aristotle, was the author of dramas intended for reading more than acting (*Rhet.* 1413ᵇ13). From the present context, however, one would assume that the *Centaur* was not a play but an epic episode (if that is what "rhapsody" implies) composed in a mixture of meters (cf. below, 1460ᵃ2). For what is meant by "all the meters" see note 5 above).

10. The nome (originally a choral song for Apollo) was hardly distinguishable in practice from the dithyramb. Large portions of Timotheus' nome *The Persians* (i.e., the Battle of Salamis) are preserved.

11. This only means that dithyramb and nome were sung by a chorus throughout, while tragedy and comedy use unsung metrical language for dialogue and song for the choral odes and other lyrical passages. All four forms obviously use language and rhythm throughout (meter being a form of rhythm— Chapter 4, 1448ᵇ21), and melody is the only difference, unless we count the special use of rhythmic dancing throughout nome and dithyramb and intermittently in tragedy and comedy.

2. DIFFERENCES ARISING FROM THE OBJECTS OF IMITATION

1. "Good men or bad." The Greek words *spoudaios* and *phaulos* are somewhat more positive, and are chosen with a view of contrasting the "objects" of tragedy and comedy—noble and serious (*spoudaioi*) persons like Philoctetes or Antigone as against common and irresponsible (*phauloi*) persons like Strepsiades (in Aristophanes' *Clouds*) or Lysistrata. The distinction is primarily ethical, but with overtones of social status. Tragedy itself is, therefore, defined (Chapter 6) as imitating a "serious" (*spoudaios*) action, since its persons are *spoudaioi;* but the ethical emphasis is clear in Chapter 15, where a less "loaded" synonym (*chrestos*) is used for these "good" characters and status is eliminated in the observation that even a slave may be good. The lowness of common characters, again, is limited in Chapter 5, where it is noted that their "badness" must stop short of being harmful or destructive. Presumably, Aristotle's intermediary characters, "men like ourselves," are on the whole "good," without being heroic; his examples, unfortunately, are lost to us, but the people of Plato's dialogues may perhaps be cited as men like ourselves.

2. All three are of the fifth century, Polygnotus being one of the greatest of Greek painters, while Pauson and Dionysius are no more than names to us. In *Politics* 8.5, 1340ᵃ36, Aristotle advises that the young should look, not at the works of Pauson but at those of Polygnotus or any other artist who expresses moral ideas. In any case, we are probably not to think of portraiture for these painters, but of "historical" scenes from myth and legend.

3. Cleophon's commonplace style is noticed below (22, 1458ᵃ20) and again in *Rhetoric* 3.7, 1408ᵃ15; he is otherwise unknown. Of Hegemon we only know that

he lived in Athens in the latter half of the fifth century. Nicochares may be a comic poet of that name, also of the late fifth century. The title *Deiliad* probably means something like "Poltrooniad."

4. Timotheus of Miletus (ca. 450-360 B.C.), famous as a musical innovator, and Philoxenus of Cythera (ca. 436-380 B.C.) were leading composers of nomes and dithyrambs. Timotheus presumably ennobled the cyclops Polyphemus, while Philoxenus' *Cyclops* or *Galatea* was reputed to be a covert satire on the tyrant Dionysius of Syracuse; it lies behind Theocritus' idyls 6 and 11. The name of a third dithyrambic or nomic poet may have been lost from the text (the Paris MS. has an unintelligible syllable *gas*); but the sentence as it stands hardly admits of this. The difference in *êthos* between the cyclopes of Timotheus and Philoxenus probably was notorious; a third cyclops "like ourselves" would have to be explicitly differentiated. The theme was, to be sure, repeatedly handled by the dithyrambic and dramatic poets—on one occasion, three cyclops dithyrambs were performed before Philip of Macedon—and the characterization no doubt varied among them.

5. The chapter begins and ends with the dual division, higher and lower characters, because Aristotle keeps in mind that he is differentiating among the arts of his original list. The tripartite division, higher, lower, and middle, imposes itself logically and is practically interesting; it could be applied to *drama:* Sophocles portrays higher men, Euripides men as they are (25, 1460ᵇ33), and Aristophanes lower types, but this would confuse the issue.

3. DIFFERENCES IN THE MANNER OF IMITATING

1. The description of "manner" is remarkably close to the interesting discussion of this subject in Plato's *Republic* 392D-394D, which Socrates summarizes as follows: "Of poetry and storytelling, there is one kind that is accomplished wholly through imitation—that is, tragedy and comedy—another wholly through narration by the poet himself—this perhaps you would find especially in dithyrambs—and still another through both imitation and narration, found in epic poetry and frequently elsewhere." By imitation Plato here means simply impersonation—what Aristotle, for whom imitation has a wider meaning, must paraphrase as "in action and functioning." Note that "manner" concerns only the form of composition, and there is no thought of actors in "acting and doing," but only of the *dramatis personae*—the play is carried on, e.g., by Clytemnestra and Agamemnon.

2. The word *drâma* ("a thing done") is in fact derived from *drân* ("to do"), plural participle *drôntes*.

3. The tyrant Theagenes is said to have been expelled from Megara around 580 B.C.

4. The Sicilian Epicharmus seems to have begun producing farces or comedies toward the end of the sixth century, but lived at least until 467 B.C. Of the Athenian poets, Chionides is said to have been active about 488 B.C. and Magnes won his first victory in 473 B.C.

5. It is hardly doubtful that "comedy" is from *kômazein*, or rather from *kômos*, a band of revelers, and *ôdê*, song. Since Aristotle is only recording the Dorian claims, the derivation of "tragedy" (apparently "goat song") does not

come up for discussion. In fact, the origin of this term remains uncertain; see A. W. Pickard-Cambridge, *Dithyramb, Tragedy, and Comedy,* 2d ed., ed. T. B. L. Webster (Oxford, 1962). A careful investigation of this controversial subject is made in Walter Burkert's article, "Greek Tragedy and Sacrificial Ritual," *Greek, Roman, and Byzantine Studies* 7 (1966):87–121.

4. THE ORIGIN OF POETRY AND THE GROWTH OF DRAMA

1. In what follows, it has been needlessly questioned whether the two causes are meant to be (1) imitative activity and (2) the enjoyment of imitations or (1) imitation in general and (2) melody and rhythm, which are also called natural. The first alternative is clearly correct, since imitation and the enjoyment of imitations are basic to Aristotle's whole theory and prominent in his mind, while melody and rhythm are of little concern to him. After explaining enjoyment of imitations at length, he turns back to the first cause, imitation (i.e., making imitations), which is his main theme. See note 3.

2. "Images" (*eikones*), i.e. plastic representations of any kind—pictures, sculpture, carved gems, etc. Aristotle regularly distinguishes animals as "noble and base" as we say "higher and lower" (cf. *Part. An.* 645ᵃ4–17). The ps.-Arist. *Magna Moralia* (1205ᵃ30) mentions as "base" animals worms and beetles; scarabs and similar replicas were no doubt valued as ornaments. Corpses would appear in paintings and reliefs of battle scenes.

3. As natural or primitive instincts leading to the creation of poetry, Aristotle has first named imitation and delight in imitations, ascribing the one to man's animal nature and the other to a natural pleasure in learning. (The latter point is made again in *Rhetoric* 1.11, 1371ᵇ4–10, where the pleasure of inferring what the imitation represents is seen as attended by pleasurable surprise.) These two causes will account for the imitative arts in general but not for poetry specifically. So he rapidly thrusts in two other causes recognized as primitive and closer to poetry, harmony and rhythm, which Plato (*Laws* 653E) had seen as distinguishing men from the animals. This addition, however, only accounts for imitative music, not poetry; so at last, under rhythm, he mentions verses (metrical language), not as a cause, since verses are not natural or primitive, but as a development from rhythm. Since, by definition, poetry is imitation in the medium of metrical language, the second natural cause would logically have been the gift of speech, but this was not available to Aristotle, since he was among those who believed that language was not natural but conventional or invented (*On Interp.* 2 and 4). The four natural causes he mentions are prior to the invention of language; with the addition of the more recently invented "verse," he completes the triad, melody, rhythm, verse, recognized as defining poetry by Plato in *Symposium* 205B and *Gorgias* 502C.

4. The *Margites,* now believed to be much later than Homer, was a burlesque epic poem with a blundering hero, who "knew many things, but knew them all badly." Only a few lines have survived, but these show that it was written in a combination of iambics and hexameters. As presently appears, it was not a genuine lampoon, but approached the generalized humor of comedy.

5. It is close to the rhythm of ordinary speech (below 1449ᵃ21–28).

6. Margites was a *typical* blunderer, and in fact the name became proverbial

in antiquity for this kind of character. For comedy as universalized humor, see Chapter 9 below.

7. The thought is put down rapidly. More clearly, no poem of the scoffing type is known before Homer; but beginning with Homer we can name the *Margites* and other such poems (these would include, for example, the poems of Archilochus). The *Margites* is still tentative in introducing iambics among hexameters, but in the others the iambic came to prevail. Such was Homer's genius, however, that his *Margites* is not only an early scoffing poem, but at the same time transcends that type in adumbrating the generalized form of comedy.

8. While tragedy, as is noted just below, now possesses its general nature (*physis*) as the direct, and not narrated, imitation of a serious action in suitable language and meter, the question is left open whether it has fully realized its possible forms or species (*eidê*). What Aristotle had in mind in *eidê* is uncertain, but the word here is probably untechnical and without anticipation of the six "parts" of tragedy (Chapter 6) or the four "species" (Chapter 18), though closer perhaps to the latter. In the abstract, he may think of the possibility of a more generalized human tragedy freed from the disabilities imposed by the traditional myths or "names" (Chapter 9 below). Mention of the audience (or the theater) may well suggest that different forms of tragedy might be developed if the conventions of presentation were altered. Thus the length of plays is dictated by the requirements of the dramatic contests, but this is no concern of the poetic art, which would perhaps better realize its aim with plays of greater length (Ch. 7 end). The *Poetics* is not primarily an analysis of the existing drama, but an inquiry into the very nature of drama, the full understanding of which may suggest better forms for its realization; but that must be left for another discussion.

9. Tragedy developed from the dithyramb or choral hymn to Dionysus (a serious form as being sacred, though apparently not solemn; see below). The chorus leader, who improvises, while the chorus no doubt answers with a fixed refrain, is regarded as the embryonic poet-actor. Comedy in turn springs from the phallic performances—processions (*kômoi*) carrying the phallus and singing indecent songs—which were also a part of the worship of Dionysus. Meanwhile, the dithyramb survives, though in altered form and no longer an improvisation, in the Attic Dionysia, and the phallic performances survive, perhaps still as improvisations, "in many places" (probably not, therefore, in Athens). Modern scholarship questions whether this view of the origin of tragedy and comedy rested on competent evidence or was no more than a reasonable conjecture; but in any case it is unlikely to have been Aristotle's personal inference, since the subject seems to have been widely discussed; cf. the Dorian claims, above, Chapter 3, 1448ª29 ff.

10. Aristotle proceeds to exemplify the "many changes" through which tragedy attained its proper nature.

11. Aristotle either assumes that the improvising chorus leader was the first actor or, more likely, merely passes over Thespis, who is often said to have introduced the first actor and spoken parts.

12. In the dramatic contests of the fifth century, each group of three tragedies was followed by a satyr play—i.e., the short and ludicrous treatment of a mytho-

logical subject, with a chorus of satyrs. Aristotle apparently regarded the satyr play as a survival representing a stage in the development of tragedy, though this belief conflicts with his account of the origins of serious poetry. However, the satyr play from which he sees tragedy emerging evidently was an early form having the spoken parts in tetrameters; in the little we have of the satyr play (Euripides' *Cyclops* and various fragments incuding about a third of Sophocles' *Ichneutae*, "The Trackers"), iambic trimeters prevail, as in tragedy, though perhaps significantly the *Ichneutae* contains tetrameters and the *Cyclops* has none.

13. These distinctions also appear in *Rhetoric* 3.8, 1408^b32 ff., where the trochaic measure, especially the rapid tetrameter, is associated with the dancing of comedy. However, when Aristotle says that the meter changed from the trochaic tetrameter to the iambic, he refers to the spoken parts; the agitated tetrameter for these parts was in harmony with the preponderance of dancing, satyrs being more addicted to dancing than to dialogue; they probably did not dance to tetrameters.

14. "Episodes" are the scenes of dramatic action separated by the choral odes. The surviving tragedies regularly have about five such scenes; the short satyr play or primitive tragedy would not have so many.

5. NOTES ON COMEDY, EPIC POETRY, AND TRAGEDY

1. The point is that we laugh at faults in conduct so long as they are harmless and not painful; when they begin to be painful and injurious it is no longer a laughing matter. The idea of the comic "error" *(hamartēma)* no doubt is in deliberate contrast to the tragic "error" *(harmartia,* below, 13, 1453^a10) of the higher type of person, which *is* painful and destructive. Since probably all the vices can be, and in the history of comedy have been, treated in the comic (harmless) manner, "the shameful" here is synonymous with "depravity" (all vice is shameful), but prepares the mind for the specific quality of the ridiculous. Though the Greek word *(aischros)* can equally well refer to disgraceful appearance (that of Thersites, for example), it is unlikely that Aristotle intends to complicate his ethical point with that notion; the comic mask is only a clever analogue. The thought seems rather to recall the discussion of comedy in Plato's *Philebus* (48A–50B), where also the ridiculous is seen as "coming under the head of badness," and is referred especially to a lack of self-knowledge (hence the comic "mistake"?), but only "the weaker sort of person" is said to be called ridiculous, for one would not dare to laugh at the powerful. For Plato here the comic always involves the "painful," and there is always malice in the laughter, but in his *Laws* 11, 934A–936B, he makes allowance for a "harmless" type of comic poem, though not, it seems, with much conviction. Aristotle, we recall, has praised Homer (above, 4, 1448^b36) for anticipating comedy by discovering the ridiculous, whereas the iambic lampoon had deliberately aimed to cause pain and provoke a blush of shame.

2. At Athens, the dramatic contests were supervised by the chief annual magistrate, the archon eponymos. Poets wishing to compete applied to him, and to those whom he selected he "granted a chorus." This means that he not only assigned the poet a chorus and actors, but appointed a *chorēgus,* that is, a wealthy citizen who would defray the expenses of the production as a public

service. The outcome of the contest was recorded in the state archives under the name of the archon. Our considerable information about these records probably goes back to Aristotle, who transcribed them from the archives, and thus transmitted them to the literary tradition (see Rudolph Pfeiffer, *History of Classical Scholarship* [Oxford, 1968], p. 81); whether the surviving inscriptions containing many of these records also depend on Aristotle's work is debated (Pickard-Cambridge, *Festivals*, p. 105). We thus know that the archon first granted a chorus for comedy in the City Dionysia of 486 B.C. That this was "late" in the development of comedy may be assumed, since Chionides at least, and perhaps Magnes and others (Chapter 3, note 4), would have become known as comic poets, employing companies of "volunteers," before they were admitted to the state contests. The term "volunteers" may be technical, since those who presented comedies at Thebes were so called (Athenaeus 14, 621b).

3. The names Epicharmus and Phormis appear at this point in the manuscripts in no grammatical relation to the sentence. Phormis was a younger contemporary of Epicharmus.

4. Crates was active between 450 and 430 B.C.

5. Chapter 2, 1446ª16. Aristotle apparently thinks of tragedy as a basic, preexistent form that epic poetry "followed" even though realized epic poems are earlier in time than realized tragedies.

6. By difference in length is meant the material length—say 1,500 lines for a tragedy and 15,000 for an epic poem, but this is restated in terms of the imagined time of the action, which obviously has a bearing on the length. The action of Sophocles' *Electra* takes place within one day, that of the *Iliad* perhaps occupies about seven weeks, but estimates vary; it is unrestricted. It is on this passage that Renaissance critics based their notion of the "unity of time"; supposing that the latter part of the sentence referred to time of presentation, they were puzzled to know how the audience could sit through "one revolution of the sun or a little more."

6. TRAGEDY DEFINED AND ANALYZED INTO PARTS

1. The procedure is in accord with that recommended in Plato's *Phaedrus* 265D–266B, whereby the scattered elements of a subject are gathered into a definition, from which logical divisions of the subject can be deduced for orderly discussion. See Introduction, p. 11

2. As carried on by "good" men, in fact men "better than the average"; see Chapter 2 and Chapter 13.

3. As appears just below, this means that metrical language alone is used in dialogue, but language fashioned to melody is used in the choruses and other lyrical parts.

4. The specific emotional effect of tragedy, gained through pity, and fear, is placed in a general category, the *catharsis* (purgation) of such emotions. The meaning is clear if we turn the sentence around: There is an effect called the "purgation" of certain emotions; tragedy produces it by means of the emotions pity and fear. (I have added the words "what we call" in brackets in the belief that the definite article, "the" *catharsis*, expresses, as often in Greek, a quasi quotation or an assumption on the writer's part that the reader is already famil-

iar with the thing mentioned.) Tragedy achieves in the spectator through its specific emotions, pity and fear, the pleasurable effect we recognize generally as the "purgation" or relief of such emotions; other arts may produce this effect through other emotions, but also some other arts—e.g., epic poetry, the dithyramb, flute music—may like tragedy produce it through pity and fear. So much is said or allowed for in Aristotle's condensed phrasing, and it is in agreement with his more extended remarks on *catharsis* in *Politics* 8 (1341^b33-1342^a29), where "a sort of purgation and pleasurable relief" is said to be the effect of "active and passionate" music on "persons subject to pity and fear *and other emotional people generally*" (cf. "such emotions"), some being especially susceptible to these emotions and all susceptible to them in some degree. Thus *catharsis* appears to be nothing but the feeling of relief that comes from giving way to the emotions in an intense emotional experience. At the end of the *Poetics* Aristotle recommends tragedy for its vividness and concentration and its music: a tragedy is a concentration, an orgy, of pity and fear, as perhaps an Aristophanic comedy is an orgy of laughter. The emotional persons specified in *Politics* 8 have been recognized by modern scholars as probably such as Aristotle would think of having a melancholic temperament (due to an excess of warm black bile) and subject to crises that could be alleviated by actual purgative drugs or by therapeutic music (as David's music relieved Saul) or by tragedy. This may be so, but in the *Politics* passage, *catharsis* is clearly a medical metaphor for an unmedical specific effect that has no name of its own (*Poet.* 21, 1457^b25), and is not necessarily to be taken literally or physically. The discharge of the emotions is in any case a temporary psychological effect without moral consequences; one does not become fearless and pitiless from attending the theater, any more than a melancholy man is permanently transformed into a jovial one by drugs or music. The spectator is not so well purged by the first tragedy at the festival as to be unable to have a similar enjoyment of the next one and those that follow, up to nine in all. Repeated tragic experiences in real life (or the real horrors of the Roman gladiatorial shows) may indeed either harden one or, on the contrary, increase one's tendency to be pitiful and timorous whence we may perhaps infer that it is because tragedy is an *imitation* that the pleasure it gives is harmless—this emotional experience has no consequences for us. It is a human instinct to enjoy imitations, even imitations of unpleasant things (Chapter 4, 1448^b4-19).

The word *catharsis*, in this sense, appears only here in the *Poetics*. Here no doubt it adds to pity and fear the necessary idea that they give pleasure, and pleasure of a harmless, psychological kind, without moral consequences. This is more useful in the definition than merely to say: "producing through pity and fear the characteristic pleasure of tragedy" (cf., e.g., 1453^b11-12); but the word is not needed again because the *Poetics* is concerned only with the means of arousing the specific emotions of pity and fear. Aristotle was probably not the first to regard these as the special emotions of tragedy (cf. Gorgias, *Helen* 8; Plato, *Phaedrus* 268). The Greek words are perhaps stronger than the English, *eleos* possibly suggesting tears and lamentation, and *phobos* something just short of terror. These emotions are dealt with in Chapters 13 and 14. On pity and fear in general, see *Rhetoric* 2.5 and 8.

5. Having viewed Tragedy as a whole, Aristotle now deduces that it has six vital parts and no more. First, since it is an imitation in direct dramatic form, it ipso facto has a visual dimension like life itself, which, as realized in theatrical production, he calls *opsis* (outward appearance or spectacle). Primarily, this will mean the outward appearance of the personages in the play, but the supposition (Bywater, Comm.; Else) that it means *only* this—i.e., the costuming of the actors and chorus—is insecurely based on the fact that Aristotle says so little about *opsis*. How do we draw the line? Is the watchman, properly costumed, spectacle at the beginning of *Agamemnon*, but not the house roof on which he reclines? or Agamemnon spectacle, but not the crimson tapestry that he treads under foot? Aristotle says little about Spectacle and Melody (music) because this treatise is about the poet's work, the poem, and spectacle and music were largely the work of the stage personnel and the musicians. But he expresses himself with care (see the end of this chapter); spectacle is the part least essential to the art of the poet, but it is not inessential; the "machine" is used at the end of Euripides' plays because the poet planned it so. For the *Poetics*, therefore, the discussion centers on the personages (their characters and thoughts), the action imitated (plot), and the language.

6. Melody (i.e. music) primarily means the singing of the choral odes and other lyrical passages. It was of very great importance in the total effect of the play (see the end of this chapter and Chapter 26, 1462^{a}15), but our information on the music of drama is limited. See J. F. Mountford in the *Oxford Classical Dictionary*, s.v. "Music," and Pickard-Cambridge, *Festivals*, pp. 262-267.

7. Reading τούτους (*toutous*) for οὖς (*hous*); cf. 1448^{a}1-2.

8. This phrase is bracketed by Kassel.

9. I. e. the Greek word *mythos* generally means a story, but Aristotle is here giving it a technical sense as the fable or plot of a play. The "action" which the plot imitates is the basic event that is being dramatized—Oedipus discovers the slayer of Laius, Orestes avenges his father's murder, Othello mistakenly slays his wife and then discovers his error. The plot is the realization of this action in a series of probable incidents, and different playwrights may invent different plots for the same action, as Aeschylus, Sophocles, and Euripides do in "imitating" the action of Orestes' revenge in the *Choephoroe* and the two Electra plays.

10. Reading ὀλίγοις (*oligois*). Within the species Tragedy every individual play will possess all the essential attributes. [Although Hutton's note gives no indication, the reading ὀλίγοις appears to be his own conjecture for this much debated passage. G.M.K.]

11. According to Aristotle, the end we aim at in life is happiness (*Nic. Eth.* 1.6, 1098^{a}16), and happiness is not a state but an activity (*ibid.* 1.10, 1101^{a}15; 10.6, 1176^{b}7; *Pol.* 1325^{a}32; cf. Plato, *Rep.* 10, 603C). The sentence is bracketed by Kassel.

12. Zeuxis of Heraclea in Magna Graecia (late fifth and early fourth centuries), one of the most famous of Greek painters. Polygnotus, above 1448^{a}b.

13. A similar point is made in Plato's *Phaedrus* 268C-269A: "What if someone went to Sophocles and Euripides and said he knew how to compose very long speeches about a small matter and very short speeches on a large one and, whenever he wished to do so, pitiful speeches and contrariwise fearful and men-

acing speeches, and so on, and thought that therefore he could give instruction in the art of tragedy? I think they would laugh at anyone who thought that tragedy was anything but the combination of these speeches put together so as to suit with one another and the whole play. . . . . So Sophocles might say that the man was displaying the preliminaries of the tragic art but not the thing itself."

14. Reversals and recognitions are defined in Chapter 11.

15. Aristotle's insistence on this point perhaps betrays the fact that he himself thinks highly of "character" (cf. the praise of Homer, Chapter 24, 1460^{a}10), but he has no doubt that without the organizing principle there is no play. Given the rather improbable "action" of the Oedipus story, Sophocles shapes the character of Oedipus as he does for the sake of making the action seem probable. For a long period, modern criticism was almost unanimous in rejecting Aristotle's views on this matter, but more recent opinion seems to have become more receptive to them; cf. Bertolt Brecht: "In regard to style of presentation, I am at one with Aristotle in believing that the plot is the heart and core of tragedy, though we differ on the purpose for which it is performed. The plot must not be a mere springboard for sundry flights into soul-searching or whatever, but must encompass everything, and everything that is done must be done for its sake, so that when the plot is ended, everything is ended" (*Antigonemodell* 5).

16. Moral choice may be expressed by action as well as by words (15, 1454^{a}19).

17. Not in the *Poetics*; cf. *On Interpretation* 16^{a}3: "Spoken words are the symbols of mental experience and written words are the symbols of spoken words."

18. Tragedy produces its effect when merely read (Chapter 26, 1462^{a}11–13).

7. THE PLOT: COMPLETENESS AND MAGNITUDE

1. In both cases, that of the minute creature and that of the huge one, we lose all sense of its ordered structure, and we lose it because of the extremes of size. Thus the only two bases for calling anything beautiful are both absent.

2. It is very unlikely that this was ever done, since the plays were not extemporized. Speakers in the law courts, however, were timed in this way.

3. We here encountered for the first time one of the fundamental principles of the *Poetics*, that tragedy involves a change of fortune, which may either be from bad to good or from good to bad. The topic is dealt with particularly in Chapter 13.

8. THE PLOT: FURTHER REMARKS ON UNITY

1. The story of Odysseus' being gashed by a boar on Mount Parnassus is in fact told in the *Odyssey* (19.392–466), and is related to the plot, since it accounts for his scar; but this fact only helps to define Aristotle's meaning here, since the tale is incidental and is not one of the events of the poem. The story of Odysseus' feigned madness is not found in the *Odyssey*.

2. The unified object is not usually something that confronts the artist in nature; the painter selects and himself composes the battle scene he imitates. In tragedy, plot is the imitation of an action, and before the poet can construct a unified plot, he must find a unified action to imitate. For this, he searches through the myths, and in this search and in the choice he makes he is already

functioning as a poet; when he finds a unified and suitable subject in myth or history, "he is its poet" (Chapter 9, 1451^{b}32). A *Heracleid* may, like the *Odyssey*, be a successful poem if the poet can find in the various adventures of Heracles a single unified action, but the danger is that he will innocently think that the name Heracles is a guarantee of unity and that selection and composition are unnecessary. The subject is carried on in the next chapter.

3. The terms used here are suggested by the parallel with a living creature.

9. POETRY REPRESENTS THE UNIVERSAL IN THE PARTICULAR

1. The careful use of comparative words should be noted. Poetry is more philosophical than history (though it makes no pretense of being as philosophical as philosophy) because it essentially seeks the probable and thus tends more toward the general or universal (though, like history, tragedy has a particular subject matter), while history tends more to the particular (though it is not without generalization) because essentially it records what has happened.

2. In real or legendary history, the names come first—what Heracles or Alcibiades did, whether it is probable or not; in poetry, the probable story is essential and the names secondary.

3. Aristophanes and the other poets of Old Comedy, though employing plots since the time of Crates (Chapter 5, 1449^{b}7) and freely inventing names (Strepsiades, etc.), still proceeded "like the iambic poets" in attacking individuals, such as Cleon, Socrates, and others; but "now," in Aristotle's time, the poets of Middle Comedy, as we call it, had learned to construct "probable" plots after the manner of tragedy, and used primarily invented or stock names. With this whole passage on "names" it is interesting to compare the well-known fragment (191) from the comedy *Poetry (Poiêsis)* by Aristotle's exact contemporary Antiphanes (ca. 388–ca. 311 B.C.): "A blessed kind of poetry is tragedy altogether. In the first place, its stories are already known to the spectators before anyone speaks. The poet need only remind them. Let him just say Oedipus, and they know the whole thing: his father Laius, his mother Jocasta, his daughters, his sons, and what he did and will have done to him. Again, if someone says Alcmeon, the whole play(?) is as good as told: that he went mad and slew his mother . . . and that Adrastus in anger will come forthwith and depart again. . . . And secondly, when the tragic poets can't find another word to say and give up defeated in the midst of their plays, they just hoist the machine like raising a finger [a sign of defeat], and the audience is perfectly satisfied. With us comic poets it is different; we have to invent everything, new names, the antecedent situation and the present one, the outcome and the starting point. If a Chremes or a Pheidon misses one of these connections, he is hissed off the stage, but it is all right for Peleus and Teucer to do so."

4. Agathon (late fifth–early fourth centuries), ranked high among the tragic poets; another of his innovations is noticed below (Chapter 18, 1456^{a}30). The dramatic setting of Plato's *Symposium* is the celebration of one of his victories. The title *Antheus* is a modern conjecture, the Greek MSS. giving *Anthos* ("Flower"), which, however, implies innovation beyond all likelihood even for Agathon.

5. See Chapter 1, note 7.

6. See Chapter 8, note 2.

7. For "simple" plots see the next chapter. As plots in which the change of fortune comes about in a succession of scenes without recognitions or reversals of situation, they are perhaps more in danger of becoming episodic than are complex plots. On Aristotle's scale, complex plots are best, simple plots less good, and episodic plots the worst—considered merely as plot structures; a given play, even though episodic—e. g., Aeschylus' *Prometheus Bound*—may be impressive for other reasons.

8. The object was to win a prize in the poetical contests, and winning prizes, Aristotle tells us elsewhere (*Rhet.* 3.1, 1403^{b}33), virtually depended on the actor's skill in oral delivery, so that in his day the actors, he says, were more important than the poets. Wise poets, therefore, had in mind the special talents of the actors whom they expected, or had arranged, to have assigned to them. But much earlier, Sophocles, according to the ancient *Life* of this poet, wrote his dramas to suit the talents (*phuseis*) of his actors. These included such stage celebrities as Tlepolemos and Callipides. Again (*Rhet.* 3.12, 1413^{b}9-12), in distinguishing between the careful written style and the style suited to the public contests and "most histrionic," Aristotle notes that the histrionic style has two varieties, the "ethical" and the "passionate," and that the actors looked for plays, and the poets for actors, with a view of these qualities. A poet would be inclined to provide a succession of scenes that would keep the famous actor on the stage in a role calculated to display his talents, even if some of these scenes were not needed for the plot and had to be improbably thrust in.

9. The same event is mentioned by Plutarch (*Moralia* 553D), who implies that it took place at a festival.

10. SIMPLE AND COMPLEX PLOTS

1. Chapters 7 and 8.

2. Recognition and Reversal are defined in the next chapter.

11. PARTS OF THE PLOT: REVERSAL, RECOGNITION, SUFFERING

1. Reversal of situation must not be confused with the overall change of fortune to good or ill, which may be embodied in a simple plot as well as in a complex one. (Reversal has not been defined before, and the words "as aforesaid" are not justified by our text of the *Poetics*.) As a feature of the complex plot, reversal need not be confined to the critical scene of a play.

2. Sophocles, *Oedipus Tyrannus* 924-1085 and 1110-1185. Aristotle summarizes too briefly. The messenger does not come with this purpose. He comes to announce that Polybus, the king of Corinth and Oedipus' supposed father, is dead and that Oedipus has been chosen to succeed him. Only after he has learned of Oedipus' fear about slaying his father and marrying his mother does he seek to rid him of it by relating the true story of his birth, which leads to the revelation that Oedipus has indeed slain his true father, Laius, and married his mother.

3. A tragedy by Aristotle's contemporary and friend, Theodectes, which is only known from this passage and Chapter 18. In the legend, Lynceus was the husband of Hypermnestra, the only one of Danaüs's daughters to spare her

husband's life in defiance of her father's orders. Despite the details mentioned in Chapter 18, it is impossible to reconstruct the plot, which clearly was one of double issue.

4. Before the recognition, the persons may be either indifferent to one another or mistakenly hostile or friendly; the recognition alters this previous attitude to the one appropriate to what is now seen to be the real situation. Electra recognizes the stranger as her brother Orestes and naturally feels affection for him; Clytemnestra recognizes him and finds herself in a situation of hostility. Recognition is the key to the complex plot and has everything to do with the happy or unhappy outcome, and hence with the emotions pity and fear. For this reason Aristotle gives preference to the recognition of persons and somewhat discounts the discovery that something has happened. It is interesting to see a modern commentator shoulder Aristotle aside: "The recognition of a person . . . is merely one special kind of this 'change from ignorance to knowledge' " (Humphry House, *Aristotle's "Poetics,"* [London, 1956], p. 97); but the mention of recognition in respect to inanimate objects and the rest "is intended to include the discovery of whole areas of circumstance, whole states of affairs, about which there was previous ignorance or mistake." If this was intended, Aristotle has expressed himself badly. To modern feeling, recognition of persons tends to seem artificial—how could Penelope fail to know her husband from the first—but for Aristotle, and probably for post-Euripidean Greek tragedy, it was central. Aristotle may have been up-to-date in inserting a whole chapter analyzing personal recognitions (Chapter 16).

5. Euripides, *Iphigeneia in Tauris* 727 ff.

6. Suffering *(pathos)*, as isolated for definition, is simply the physical pain manifested by the tragic personages on the stage. Since actual violence was avoided in the theater, and yet death in Greek tragedy is generally violent, few of its deaths could be openly enacted. In the extant plays, only Alcestis and Hippolytus die before our eyes, the one gently, from sickness, the other from violence already done behind the scenes; Ajax in Sophocles' play dies, probably, just out of sight. The tragic incident or deed of horror, described in Chapter 14 as a prime source of pity and fear, may not always be productive of "suffering." Agonies of pain are manifested by Philoctetes and Heracles; Oedipus and others appear with blinded eyes; we see the wounded charioteer of Rhesus. Fourth-century tragedy may have repaid a decline in *êthos* with a rise in suffering. But see Chapter 18, note 3.

12. THE QUANTITATIVE PARTS OF TRAGEDY

1. Chapter 12 interrupts the sequence of thought which proceeds from the definitions of the parts of plot in Chapter 11 to the proper construction of plots in Chapter 13; but the first sentence of Chapter 13 acknowledges the presence of Chapter 12.

2. Songs sung by the actors alone without the chorus.

3. Anapaestic and trochaic rhythms, suited to marching and dancing, are characteristic of the entrance song or Parodos, and Anapaests occur in other less extended utterances of the chorus.

13. THE BEST FORM OF TRAGEDY

1. The discussion of tragic plots in Chapters 10 and 11.

2. Human sympathy *(to philanthrôpon)*, as appears from the next sentence, may be felt for an evil man who deservedly suffers calamity. It seems to be an extenuated form of pity, which recognizes that the bad man is nevertheless human and to that extent like ourselves. Below (Chapter 18, 1456ᵃ21), the term is extended to allow the villain certain virtues—intelligence and courage—and it seems there to be admitted that plays featuring such characters may be effective though they are not true tragedies.

3. Pity and fear are here very adroitly defined for the purposes of the *Poetics*, as may be seen by comparing the extended description of these emotions in *Rhetoric* 2.5 and 8. The two emotions form a pair (though note that in the *Rhetoric* fear excludes pity) since they tend to be different reactions to the same kind of event: "In general, whatever people fear for themselves makes them feel pity when it happens to others" (*Rhet.* 2, 1386ᵃ27). In witnessing a tragedy, we respond directly with pity for good persons suffering what they do not deserve to suffer; we do not so directly fear for ourselves, but we have a genuine fear because we see a dreadful thing happening to someone like ourselves, someone with whom we identify ourselves—if it happened to a monster of iniquity, we would feel no fear, only satisfaction.

4. In a tragedy, the personages have the characters they have for the sake of the plot (1450ᵃ20 ff.). For the best plot—one best evoking pity and fear—the personages should be "good," but not so perfectly good as to be unlikely to make mistakes, and indeed great mistakes. Such a mistake or error of judgment Aristotle calls a *hamartia*, and the resulting deed a *hamartêma*. In the *Ethics (E. N.* 5.10, 1135ᵇ12), such mistaken acts are said to be due not to vice or depravity, but to ignorance of some relevant fact or circumstance, and since the harm they do is not intended by the doer, we pardon or pity him (*E. N.* 3.2, 1110ᵇ31). Yet since they are done intentionally, they are not mere accidents, but involve some degree of responsibility, as is shown by the fact that the doer regrets them and blames himself (*E. N.* 3.2, 1110ᵇ17 ff.). For the sake of probability, they should also be the sort of thing a certain kind of person is likely to do in the circumstances (*Poet.* Chapter 9, 1451ᵇ8). Thus in *Oedipus Tyrannus*, Oedipus' *hamartia* or mistake is the slaying of a man who might be his father but whose relationship to himself he does not know, and this after warning from the oracle that he was destined to slay his father. This mistake might seem incredible had not Sophocles provided Oedipus with the hasty and irascible temper that makes it probable that he would act thus in circumstances of extreme provocation. Such an error would be less conceivable for Homer's Odysseus, who, however, makes *his* great mistake in boasting of his own cleverness to the wrong person at the wrong time in ignorance of Polyphemus's powerful connections. Aristotle seems primarily to think of the ignorance on which the error rests as being ignorance of a personal relationship: see the next chapter (14). An error having awful consequences not intended by the tragic person may appear as something marvelous, and, especially in earlier drama, as a "blindness" attributable to divine influence *(Atê)*. The dramatists—e.g., Sophocles in *Ajax*, Euripides in *Hera-*

cles and the *Bacchae*, and apparently Astydamas in his *Alcmeon*—seem often to have relied on madness to account for this destructive error.

5. The same error as those commit who contend that the double ending is best. The polemic note in this chapter is striking, but we cannot identify the critics Aristotle opposes. The exaggerations, "most of his plays" and "faulty in everything else," may be quasi quotations.

14. HOW TO AROUSE PITY AND FEAR

1. It is still within the poet's art, since he plans the spectacular effect; but it is the less so in that its final success depends on the *skeuopoios* who provides the necessary props. See the end of Chapter 6 (1450^{b}18). Aristophanes regards the poet as responsible for spectacle when he ridicules Euripides for clothing Telephus and others in rags to make them seem pitiful. Indeed Aristotle himself seems to urge something of the sort upon the orator who aims to inspire pity (see Chapter 17, note 2). The creation of fear through spectacle is readily exemplified by the Erinyes in Aeschylus' *Eumenides*.

2. The portentous or monstrous *(teratôdes)* no doubt refers particularly to the monstrous figures, Gorgons, Harpies, and the like, that were an essential part of many Greek myths and a natural source of spectacular effect in drama. The downright statement "*not* terrifying but *only* portentous" (or monstrous), seems to exempt Aeschylus' Erinyes from this charge, since they are in fact terrifying; but Aristotle may have had Aeschylus in mind as one who notoriously aimed at striking effects gained through such figures. The ancient *Life* of Aeschylus asserts: "He used spectacle and plot [or myth] more for the portentously astounding effect than for dramatic illusion *(apatê)*." But in the loss of most of Greek tragedy, we do not know what we have missed—among other portents, "Euhippe the daughter of Cheiron changing into a horse in Euripides" (Pollux quoted by Bywater, Comm., p. 221).

3. In *Oedipus Tyrannus*, Laius is slain by Oedipus before the play begins. Astydamas the Elder (his son also was a tragic poet) was a somewhat older contemporary of Aristotle; he was a collateral descendent of Aeschylus. In this play Alcmeon probably slew his mother Eriphyle in a fit of madness and then recovered his senses (T. B. L. Webster "Fourth Century Tragedy and the Poetics," *Hermes* 82 [1954]:305). The *Odysseus Wounded* was a play of Sophocles. Telegonus, Odysseus' son by Circe, comes to Ithaca in search of his father, is mistaken for a marauder, and in the ensuing fight wounds Odysseus mortally.

4. Since in the next sentence Aristotle mentions a fourth possibility, some editors believe that it should also be inserted above.

5. Sophocles, *Antigone* 1232 ff.

6. A lost play by Euripides.

7. Both author and theme are unknown.

8. We are inclined to demur at Aristotle's choice of this last situation as the best, since when the would-be injurer desists there will be no tragic "suffering," just as in the first and worst situation, and an unhappy ending cannot follow it with probability. Yet in itself this type no doubt is the most satisfactory and thrilling, and certainly in *Iphigeneia* it furnishes one of the most enthralling scenes in literature. We might think the preceding type in which the deed is

done and the recognition follows would be more completely tragic; but in itself this arrangement has the defect of the loose end—the slayer discovers his mistake, but the slain man never knows what happened to him. This may be why Aristotle admits that *Oedipus Tyrannus* is not just what he has in mind, the murder being outside the play, and adds two normal cases in which it is within the play. In *Oedipus*, the murder of Laius rather appears as something that happened to Oedipus, but if Laius had been in the play (as Eriphyle and Odysseus were), we would have some interest in him, too. It may be significant that in three plays in which this form is used—Euripides' *Heracles* and *Bacchae* and, apparently, Astydamas' *Alcmeon*—the deed is or was done in a fit of madness; moreover in the *Bacchae* 1115 ff. we are informed that Pentheus recognized his slayer. This touch in the *Bacchae* and the exclusion of Laius from *Oedipus* are what might better be cited as examples of how to use the traditional stories "well."

9. Chapter 13, 1453ª19.

15. THE CHARACTERS OF TRAGEDY

1. The precise meaning of this sentence is uncertain, but the general sense is clear.

2. "Lifelike"—the word *homoios* is used here much as in Chapter 2, 1448ª6, Dionysius painted men "as they are in reality," and in Chapter 13, 1453ª5, we fear for men "like ourselves." A character might be represented as noble and possessing manly courage, and yet fail to be natural and convincing.

3. "Unnecessary baseness" is baseness not required by the plot. In stipulating that the characters of tragedy be "good," Aristotle apparently disregards plots of double issue, perhaps as an inferior type; the baseness of the suitors in the *Odyssey* is necessary for the plot. In Euripides' *Orestes*, it is essential to the plot that Menelaus should fail to support Orestes when the latter is prosecuted for the murder of Clytemnestra, but his treachery in first promising to help (682 ff.) and then not even turning up for the trial (1056 ff.) is unnecessary. The first Argument to this play remarks that, except Pylades, all the characters are "bad" (*phauloi*). Cf. Chapter 25, 1461ᵇ21, below.

4. *Scylla* was a dithyramb by Timotheus, not a tragedy; Odysseus' lament was for his men whom Scylla devoured. The speech of Melanippe in Euripides' (lost) *Melanippe the Wise*, was notorious for its incongruous use of scientific knowledge. Presumably Odysseus' lament seemed unmanly and Melanippe's speech unwomanly.

5. Euripides, *Iphigeneia in Aulis* 1211–52 compared with 1368–1401, where she heroically welcomes death.

6. "From the machine" means "by divine intervention" (cf. Horace's *deus ex machina*), since in the Greek theater gods were suspended over the scene by means of the *mêchanê* or crane. At the end of Euripides' *Medea*, the heroine is saved in a flying chariot of the Sun God drawn by dragons. In the *Iliad* (2.110–206), an evil dream sent by Zeus inspires Agamemnon to command the Greeks to sail for home, but Athena inspires Odysseus to prevent this. The outcome here is hardly a denouement in the dramatic sense, and it has been thought that "*Iliad*" may be a mistake for the title of a play.

7. It appears from Chapter 24 that Aristotle has in mind the unlikelihood of Oedipus' remaining so long ignorant of how Laius lost his life.

8. The Greek text is uncertain. It has been emended to secure the meaning: "As Homer represents Achilles as good *(agathon)* and an example of harshness."

9. Presumably in his dialogue *On Poets.* However, as Else seems to have been the first to observe (p. 483), this matter of the "sense perceptions" dovetails into the beginning of Chapter 17, where it is spelled out. The train of thought is interrupted by Chapter 16, which is on a different subject, and plainly there must have been a stage in Aristotle's poetry lectures, before Chapter 16 was thrust in, when Chapter 15 ran smoothly into Chapter 17.

16. DIFFERENT KINDS OF RECOGNITION *(anagnorisis)*

1. In Chapter 11.

2. "The lance the earth-born bear" is thought to be a quotation from the *Antigone* of Astydamus (341 B. C.). The earth-born are the descendants of the men who sprang from earth when Cadmus sowed the dragon's teeth. All evidently bore a birthmark resembling a lance, and in the play, Creon recognized his grandson, the son of Haemon and Antigone, by this mark (see Webster, *Hermes,* 1954, p. 305). Similarly, the descendants of Pelops had a star on their shoulders derived from Pelops' ivory shoulder. Carcinus the Younger was also a fourth-century tragic poet, apparently a little older than Astydamas.

3. A play by Sophocles. Tyro, daughter of Salmoneus, persecuted by her stepmother Sidero, had set adrift in a boat the twin sons she had secretly borne to Poseidon. These, saved by a herdsman, who named them Pelías and Neleus, and grown to manhood, were recognized by their mother by means of the boat, which apparently had been preserved. They then avenged her wrongs by slaying Sidero.

4. In the *Odyssey* 19.386 ff., Odysseus is unexpectedly recognized by Eurycleia when she bathes him; in the *Odyssey* 21.193 ff., he announces his identity to the herdsmen and displays the scar in proof.

5. Once Iphigeneia becomes known to Orestes through the letter, it is inevitable or probable that he should simply announce who he is. Aristotle seems to object to the somewhat arbitrary proofs he offers (appeals to memory).

6. Evidently Philomela, whose tongue had been cut out, revealed who did this to her by embroidering the facts in a tapestry.

7. Dicaeogenes was a tragic and dithyrambic poet of the end of the fifth century and beginning of the fourth. The *Cyprians* may have dramatized the return of Teucer from Cyprus to Salamis, and he may have been recognized when he wept at the sight of the picture of his father Telamon.

8. *Odyssey* 8.83 ff., 521 ff.

9. *Choephori* 168–234. The reasoning is that of Electra.

10. Polyidus the Sophist is unknown. As reported here, his *anagnorisis* for Iphigeneia might have been proposed in a criticism of the scene in Euripides' play, but as noticed again below (Ch. 17) it might have occurred in a poem of his own. There was a well-known dithyrambic poet Polyidus (end of the fifth century–beginning of the fourth century).

11. For Theodectes, see Chapter 11, note 3. No situation in the story of Tydeus (the father of Diomedes) fits the words here quoted.

12. This play is otherwise unknown. In all the foregoing instances, obviously the utterance of the inference mentioned led to a recognition and presumably to the salvation of the persons making it (the best kind of situation according to Chapter 14).

13. The Greek text gives "by the audience" *(theatrou)*, which is possible, but the preceding examples of recognition have all been viewed from within the play, and hence Hermann's conjecture *(thaterou)* here translated seems more likely to be correct.

14. Presumably the title of a tragedy.

15. I.e., in the play he did not actually string the bow. The interpretation of this obscure passage can only be tentative. It seems that the one sure proof of Odysseus' identity was assumed to be that he alone of all men could string the bow; but this might be hard to show in a convincing scene. Hence a second hypothesis was employed—he said he would recognize the bow. The translation assumes that when he identified it (either by describing it correctly or by choosing it among several others), this was accepted as insuring that he (alone) could string the bow. But the inference is false, since, though the person (Odysseus) who could string the bow could of course recognize it, there is no certainty that any chance person who could recognize the bow could string it. For another example of false inference, see Chapter 24, 1460ª18-26.

17. PRACTICAL HINTS FOR PLAYWRIGHTS

1. The play is unknown, and it is impossible to be sure what Carcinus' blunder was. In the legend, Amphiaraus took refuge in the temple in order to avoid joining the expedition against Thebes, but was betrayed into leaving the sanctuary by his wife Eriphyle. It has been suggested that Carcinus forgot to place him in the temple before he brought him out; or he may have appeared before the palace when he was still supposedly in the temple. Plays may have been rehearsed without a stage setting.

2. The single word "gestures" *(schêmata)* is probably a short way of saying "with dramatic action," which would include the emotional delivery of dialogue. This perhaps may be inferred from a fuller statement in the *Rhetoric* (2.8, 1386ª32); in raising sympathy for persons remote in time or place, "those orators are necessarily more piteous who work up their description with appropriate gestures, tones of voice, dress, and all that belongs to the art of acting." The assumption apparently is that in this way the poet will necessarily put himself into the emotional state of his characters, and will avoid emotions that are inappropriate. For the effect of gestures (bodily movements), see Chapter 1, 1447ª27, and Chapter 26.

3. Since emotional facility is an advantage for the production of good (dramatic and epic) poetry, Aristotle can explain on rational grounds why two types of personality, the *euphueis* (talented, able, brilliant) and the *manikoi* (mad, unstable, passionate), succeed in this art, the first being *euplastoi* (versatile, impressionable, adaptable) and the second *ekstatikoi* (excitable, apt to let them-

selves go; in *Nichomachean Ethics* 7.1–3 the word is associated with lack of self-control). These two types of personality are also connected in *Rhetoric* 2.15, 1390ᵇ28, where we learn that, when families degenerate, "brilliant" *(euphua)* stocks become "rather unbalanced" *(manikôtera)*, like the descendants of Alcibiades (sedate families become dull and stolid like the descendants of Socrates). In the pseudo-Aristotelian *Problems* (30.1, 954ª31), both *euphueis* and *manikoi* personalities are ascribed to an excess of hot, black bile (together with erotic natures, those easily moved to passion and desire, and the talkative). Clearly, these two types of character were thought to have something in common. It is even possible for Aristotle to use *manikos* as meaning no more than "passionate"; *Rhetoric* 1.9, 1367ª37, "the choleric and the passionate *(manikos)* man may be called 'outspoken.' " In the present passage, however, there is obviously an allusion to the Greek commonplace, exploited ambiguously by Plato in *Phaedrus* and *Ion*, that poets are "mad," but for Aristotle the term is psychological and without any thought of divine inspiration; the *manikos* is simply one type of personality.

Many critics have found it hard to believe that Aristotle would be so impartial, and have accepted a simple operation on the text (the insertion of *mallon*, "more," "rather") which produces the meaning "art of a man of genius *rather than* of one with a touch of madness." But the problem probably arises from too narrow an interpretation of "madness." The emphasis of Aristotle's sentence is on the explanatory words. If preference for the *euplastoi* were intended, one would expect *ekstatikoi* to indicate a trait less favorable to emotional facility; instead, it is clearly chosen precisely because it indicates emotional facility. It is not unlikely that, as he makes his dramatic gestures, an *ekstatikos* may excite himself more quickly and strongly than a *euplastos*.

4. Here the words "outside the general plan" are omitted in the translation.

5. The purpose of the outline clearly is to make sure that the plot is consistent (probable or necessary), and this is best done by omitting the traditional names at this point.

6. Apparently a slip for *Iphigeneia*. Aristotle evidently thinks of Orestes and his recognition as the center of this play.

18. MISCELLANEOUS OBSERVATIONS

1. On this play see Chapter 11. The child presumably is Abas, son of Lynceus and Hypermnestra. If the change of fortune began with the indictment (of Lynceus?) for murder, this crucial episode probably also included the peripety described in Chapter 11.

2. This reference to the "parts" *(merê)* is unintelligible. The four types of tragedy here distinguished cannot be linked with the six constituent elements of Chapter 6, or with any four of them, nor with the parts of the plot mentioned in Chapter 11. The terms on which they are based, complex plot, suffering, character, and simple plot (if this is intended), have been defined. See the parallel division of epic poems in Chapter 24 below.

3. Besides the extant *Ajax* of Sophocles, there were plays with this title by Carcinus, Theodectes, and Astydamas; there were plays about Ixion by Aeschylus and Euripides. It is difficult to decide whether *pathêtikê* means tragedy

"of suffering" or tragedy "of passion," that is, whether *pathos* should be understood in the technical sense of suffering as defined in Chapter 11 or in the broader sense, found elsewhere in the *Poetics*, of emotion or passion. It may seem decisive for "suffering" that for the corresponding *pathētikē* epic in Chapter 24, there is pointed reference to Chapter 11 (reversals, recognitions, and sufferings). Favoring "passion," on the other hand, is the likelihood that "pathetic" tragedy forms a contrasting pair with the following "ethical" tragedy. Lucas (*Comm.*, p. 187) effectively adduces *Rhetoric* 3.12, 1413ᵇ10 (see Chapter 9, note 8), which suggests that the distinction between "pathetic" (passionate) and "ethical" plays was a familiar one and corresponded to the style and ability of different actors, some being skilled in representing passion and others character. No doubt "suffering" and "passion" go closely together; a highly passionate play would be productive of open signs of suffering (Sophocles' Ajax commits suicide almost before our eyes). The stories of Ajax and Ixion are of this kind; Ajax goes mad and commits atrocities, Ixion atrociously murders his wife's father and goes mad. In Sophocles' play, there would be employment for a passionate actor as Ajax and an ethical one as Odysseus.

4. The *Phthiotides* and *Peleus* were plays by Sophocles; there was also a *Peleus* by Euripides. Tragedy of character or ethical tragedy probably means tragedy in which character delineation in the broad sense predominates, as in Polygnotus' style of painting (1450ᵃ28). See the preceding note.

5. Unfortunately the name of the fourth kind of tragedy has disappeared from the text. One might regard it as easily restored from Chapter 24, 1459ᵇ7-9, where Aristotle says that epic poetry has the same four kinds as tragedy, and names one kind as "simple"—i.e., of simple plot (above, 1452ᵃ14-16). Certainly, *Prometheus*, if the reference is to Aeschylus' play, is "simple," since the change of fortune takes place without reversal or recognition. The *Daughters of Phorcys* was a satyr play by Aeschylus, and in general Aeschylus seems to have favored simple plots. Since simple plays exist, the category "complex" would seem necessarily to entail a category "simple." Nevertheless, many scholars have preferred Bywater's suggestion that the fourth kind of tragedy is the "spectacular," since the examples cited might well all have this character, and Aristotle has admitted (Chapter 14) that the tragic effect may be produced by spectacle. Probably, however, we should abide by "simple." Despite Aristotle's preference, poems of simple plot often rouse the profounder emotion; the simple *Iliad* is more impressive than the complex *Odyssey*, and *Agamemnon* is more impressive than *Iphigeneia in Tauris*.

6. The playwright should be skilled in composing plays of different types. Homer succeeded fully in encompassing all four types in his two poems (Chapter 24, 1459ᵇ7), and presumably a playwright might make similar combinations.

7. The words here translated "compare tragedy with tragedy" literally mean "to say a tragedy is other and the same." Fundamental to the existence of Greek tragedy was the rehandling of the same stories by different dramatists, each with his own treatment of plot and other points of technique. We are still in a position to say how the tragedy of Orestes and Clytemnestra is "other and the same" in the versions of Aeschylus, Sophocles, and Euripides; but for Aristotle

the field of tragedy was a mass of plays on the same themes. And in his own day such comparison was inevitable, since the poets had narrowed their choice of subjects to "only a few houses" (Chapter 13, 1453ª14; Chapter 14, 1454ª9). For one feature *(meros)*, compare Euripides' handling of the recognition of Orestes in the Iphigeneia tragedy with the improvement devised by Polyidus (Chapter 16, 1455ª6).

8. The point has not been made explicitly, but see Chapters 5 and 17; cf. Chapters 23 and 26.

9. The *Sack of Troy* was the title of a (lost) epic poem; it is not certain, however, that Aristotle uses the words as a title here. The theme provided Euripides with subjects for *Hecuba, The Trojan Woman,* and a (lost) *Epeus.* Aeschylus' *Niobe,* of which important fragments remain, was among his most famous plays; but it is not clear why it should be mentioned here, and the text may be faulty. Apparently, it was not uncommon for plays to be hissed off the stage; see Pickard-Cambridge, *Festivals,* pp. 272–273.

10. See Chapter 13 on the poet's "aim," and especially 1452ª38–53ª3 for "human sympathy." Agathon's comment occurred in a play, and is quoted in its original form in Aristotle's *Rhetoric* 2.24, 1402ª10: "Perhaps someone may say that this is itself probable, that many things may befall mortals that are not probable." It seems probable, or at least appropriate, that a clever villain should be outwitted.

11. Since an actor is one who has a role in the dramatic action, the dramatist is advised to think of the chorus as having such a role among the other actors and not as a completely detached body of singers as evidently they had come to be in Aristotle's day. Having a role in the performance is equivalent to being involved in the plot of the play, and Aristotle thinks the choruses of Sophocles are better integrated into the play than those of Euripides. To mention the importance of the chorus in Aeschylus here would serve no practical purpose.

12. Presumably these include younger contemporaries of Sophocles and Euripides.

19. THOUGHT AND LANGUAGE

1. Actually only Plot and Character have been discussed; Spectacle and Music, though elements of tragedy, are not strictly within the "method" of *poiêtikê;* the poet's design may call for certain effects of spectacle and music, but the art of the property man and that of the musician supply them. The element of Thought is indeed important in the composition of a poem, but it more properly belongs to the art of rhetoric and is treated by Aristotle under that art. Only Language remains to be discussed in the *Poetics.*

2. The reference presumably is to Books 1 and 2 of the *Rhetoric,* where both argumentation and the treatment of the emotions are discussed at length. In what follows, Aristotle is content to touch only on aspects of Thought that may be especially pertinent to drama. The "effects" are primarily efforts of one character to persuade or move other characters in the play.

3. Thought is properly an aspect of the speeches in the dialogue of a play, in which the characters present arguments, stir emotions, or make general observations (Chapter 6, 1449ᵇ38; 1450ᵇ4–14), and in these functions speeches in drama

do not essentially differ from speeches in the assembly or law courts. But a play is a direct imitation of life, and it is in point here, therefore, to mention that, as in life (and more freely than in oratory), Thought can be expressed in actions as well as in words. The distinction is drawn sharply. If a thought is to be expressed by an action, the action must convey it independently of language; if a thought is to be expressed by language, the language, and the language alone, must convey it. No doubt Thought in relation to the major action of a play—e.g., Orestes' revenge on Clytemnestra—is usually put into the speeches, and the role of actions without verbal explanation will be relatively minor. Nevertheless, it is important, since Greek tragedy, like life, abounds in such actions. To perform an act "without verbal explanation" presumably does not mean that the doer of the act must say nothing, only that the thought must primarily take effect in the act. Cassandra throws her garland and her wand to the ground and crushes them, and it is the act that expresses her thought, not the statement that accompanies it (*Agam.* 1264-8). But very often the doer says nothing at all, and readers of a play only know of the act from the persons affected. "Here you, what are you doing?" (the king to the herald, who evidently has started to lay hands on the maidens, Aesch., *Suppl.* 909). "Keep your hands off me" (Hippolytus to the nurse, who evidently has touched his garment in supplication, Eur., *Hipp.* 605); viewers of Euripides' *Hecuba* (438-501) see the queen lying prostrate on the ground throughout a fairly long scene, readers only learn that this is so when Talthybius asks where she is and the chorus answers. (The word "independently" represents the translator's correction ἰδίᾳ [*idiâi*] for the manuscript reading ἡδέα [*hêdea*], "sweet.")

4. The forms of expression or types of sentences (first distinguished by Protagoras in the fifth century) are dismissed by Aristotle in *On Interpretation* (4, 17ᵃ5-8), a logical work, as belonging rather to poetics or rhetoric; here in the *Poetics* they are handed on to the art of elocution or dramatic delivery, since they involve intonation. In the *Rhetoric* (3.1, 1403ᵇ25), we are told that the art of dramatic delivery had been systematized by Glaucon of Teos and others.

5. The first line of the *Iliad*.

6. Protagoras of Abdera (ca. 485-ca. 415), one of the leading Sophists.

20. LANGUAGE IN GENERAL: DEFINITIONS

1. In three short chapters Aristotle now gives an efficient account of the Language of poetry, proceeding, somewhat as in the case of poetry itself, from language in general to the specific forms used by poets and ending with observations on how these should be treated if the poetry is to be good. Especially illuminating are his remarks on metaphor and his definition of a distinguished style as a blend of familiar and unfamiliar elements. Somewhat later, he returned to the subject of style in the third book of the *Rhetoric*, which deserves to be read in connection with this part of the *Poetics*.

The present chapter on language in general reads like an independent study, perhaps not originally designed for the *Poetics*. It finds that language has eight "parts," the definitions of which seem to have been established by a Platonic division of *diaeresis* recalling the *diaeresis* of language sketched by Plato in the *Philebus* 18B (A. von Fragstein, *Die Diairesis bei Aristoteles* [*Amsterdam*,

1967]). The chapter is of historical interest in being, with a shorter sketch in the treatise *On Interpretation,* the earliest treatment of formal Greek grammar that survives. The study of language had been initiated in the fifth century by the Sophists, particularly by Protagoras, Prodicus, and Hippias; Democritus seems to have written on the subject; Plato's *Cratylus* handles it philosophically; but the principal advances were made after Aristotle's time by the Stoics. Finally, grammar, as it has been known in the West until very recent times, was formulated in the second century B.C. by Dionysius Thrax, whose work survives. See Rudolph Pfeiffer, *The History of Classical Scholarship* (Oxford, 1968), Chapters 2-3.

2. By "letter" Aristotle here means the sound and not the written symbol. The word translated as "unified utterance" is *logos,* which, as defined by Aristotle below in accordance with Greek usage, includes every significant combination of words from the single phrase or sentence to the complete poem or oration. The word translated as "article" (*arthron,* "joint") is the regular word for the definite article in later Greek grammarians, but as defined below it cannot mean this here, nor is any meaning conveyed by the definition.

3. Possibly a reference to the work of the Sophist Hippias, who is known to have treated "letters," syllables, etc., in connection with music. See Pfeiffer, *op. cit.,* p. 53.

4. The Greek text is faulty; Bywater's interpretation is here followed. In this interpretation both sentence connectives, like English "and," "but," and prepositions are called connective particles.

5. The Noun (lit. "name") includes adjectives and perhaps pronouns.

6. Evidently any meaningful modification, whether indicated by the form of the word or by intonation in uttering the same form, is an inflection (*ptôsis,* English "case"). Modes of utterance are also noticed above, 1456[b]8-13. Since Greek had no mark of interrogation in Aristotle's time, a reader would gather from the context what intonation to give to "walked."

7. Aristotle frequently gives definitions of man (see the Index in the Oxford [Ross] translation of the *Categories,* etc. s.v. "man"), but the one given in *On Interpretation* 5, 17[a]13, "a footed animal with two feet," many be meant here, since the linguistic matter in *On Interpretation* resembles that in the *Poetics* and the phrase is also said to be a unified utterance.

8. A verb, such as "walks," is a significant sound, but does not have independent meaning; it must be said of something (*On Interp.* 3, 16[b]8-25).

21. LANGUAGE IN GENERAL: CLASSIFICATION OF WORDS

1. The term here translated as "word" is *onoma,* which Aristotle has used technically in Chapter 20 in the sense of "noun," distinguishing it from *rhêma,* "verb." Here it reverts to its general sense and includes both nouns and verbs.

2. Since prepositions are "nonsignificant" (1457[a]4), all words compounded with them fall into the first class (e.g., "amphitheater"); the second class is illustrated by "Theodore" ("god" + "gift") 1457[a]13.

3. Instead of "the people of Marseilles," the Greek manuscripts have a corrupted word, which has been emended to give the meaning "(Most of) the grandiose names." All recent editors, however, follow H. Diels (*Sitzungsb. Berlin. Akad.* [Berlin, 1888], I, 53) in adopting the reading of the Arabic version

translated here, especially since the name Hermo-caico-Xanthus combines the names of three rivers not far from Phocaea in Asia Minor, which was the city from which Marseilles was settled. Accompanying the name in the Arabic translation are words meaning "who prays to the lord of heaven" (i.e., Zeus). The name Hermocaicoxanthus would fit into a hexameter verse, and it is less absurd to imagine with Diels that a comic poem is referred to than to understand, as others do, "most (softened to 'many') of the names of the people of Marseilles" or "most (many) of the words in the Marseilles dialect."

4. The Arabic version seems to show that this was completed with something like "and *doru* is the current word with us but foreign in Cyprus."

5. *Odyssey* 1.185 and 24.308.

6. *Iliad* 2.272.

7. The quotations are probably from Empedocles' *Purifications* (frgs. 138 and 143 Diels). The first may refer to the slaughter of a sacrificial animal; in the second, Aristotle omits to say what is "cut off," but the same quotation (it seems) in fragment 143 suggests that it is the water "from five springs."

8. In the proportion A:B = C:D, metaphor consists in calling B by the name of D and vice versa. Thus, in the second example below, old age (A):life (B) = evening (C):day (D), and by substituting day (D) for life (B) we get "the old age of the day" as a metaphor for evening, and by substituting life (B) for day (D) we get "the evening of life" for old age.

9. The proportion here is to be inverted: Dionysus (A) in relation to the cup (B) is analogous to Ares (C) in relation to the shield (D). The metaphors consist in calling the wine cup a shield and the shield a wine cup, and are completed in each case by adding "of Ares" (C) and "of Dionysus" (A), the related terms in the analogy to the proper (unmetaphorical) terms "shield" (D) and cup (B). The metaphor "wine cup of Ares" for "shield" is found in Timotheus' *The Persians*, frg. 22 Wilamowitz.

10. The words of Empedocles have not been preserved.

11. From an unknown poet.

12. The discussion of the Ornamental word, which, according to the list in 1457b1, should come at this point, is lost. It seems fairly certain, however, that it included a treatment of synonyms, with examples to show how one may choose among several synonymous words that which is the most beautiful or suitable. And in fact we are informed by Simplicius, the ancient commentator on Aristotle's *Categories* (*Cat.* 36.13 Kalbfleisch), that synonyms were dealt with in the *Poetics* (as is not now the case): "In the *Poetics*, Aristotle said that synonyms are words more than one in number but having the same meaning . . . , for example, mantle, cloak, cape." Compare *Rhetoric* III, 2, 1404b37: "Homonyms are useful to the sophist, . . . synonyms to the poet." The discussion that follows in *Rhetoric* 1405a1 ff., though centered on metaphor, contains points and examples that may well have appeared here in the *Poetics*—e.g., "It makes a difference whether we say 'rosy-fingered dawn' or 'crimson-fingered' or, still worse, 'red-fingered.' "

13. The word *ernygas* is unknown; but *arêtêr* appears in *Iliad* 1.11 and 5.78. Here, as often, "the poet" may mean Homer.

14. All the preceding "expanded" and "curtailed" forms occur in Homer.

15. Empedocles, frg. 88 Diels ("there comes to be one vision of both [eyes]").

16. *Iliad* 5.393 ("on the right breast").

17. The genders properly speaking are only masculine and feminine; but there are many nouns that are neither (neuter), which Aristotle here calls "intermediate" presumably because they share in masculine and feminine endings. The classification of nouns by gender seems to have been introduced by Protagoras (Aristotle, *Rhet.* 3.5, 1407^{b}8). He called neuters *skeuê*—i.e., "thing words."

18. The list is not quite exact, since there are a few feminine words ending in sigma. It is exact for proper names, and on these the classification probably was founded (Bywater, Comm.). The terminations, of course, are those of the nominative singular.

19. This list is omitted in the best Greek MSS. [Angle brackets are used in classical texts to indicate words that do not appear in the manuscripts of the text but are supplied from other ancient sources, as here, or by editorial conjecture, as on pages 75 and 77. G.M.K.] It appears, at least in part, in the Arabic version, and, as given here, was written (ca. 1498) by Georgio Valla in the margin of his MS.; but probably in both instances it was derived from a Greek grammar and not from the text of Aristotle (See E. Lobel, *The Greek Manuscripts of Aristotle's Poetics* [London, 1933], pp. 25, 36). Still, some of these words must have been in Aristotle's mind, since nouns with this ending are actually few in number though more than five (e.g., add *dakru*, tear).

20. The statement is incomplete, since neuter nouns also end in rho and short alpha. The neuter nouns thus share all the endings of the masculine and short alpha among the endings of the feminine, while a limited number of them have peculiar endings in omicron and upsilon.

22. THE LANGUAGE OF POETRY

1. I.e., "language" (*lexis*) in the sense of "style," but style considered only in respect to vocabulary as analyzed in Chapter 20. In the more extended treatment of style in Book 3 of the *Rhetoric*, distinctions are made between the style of poetry and that of prose.

2. Cleophon, Chapter 2, 1448^{a}12; Sthenelus is probably the tragic poet whose poor style is mentioned by Aristophanes (*Gerytades*, frg. 151; cf. *Wasps* 1313).

3. In proper terms: I saw a doctor applying to a patient a heated cupping instrument made of bronze (for the purpose of bleeding the patient). The riddle is sometimes ascribed to Cleobulina, who was famous for her riddles. Aristotle cites it again in *Rhetoric* 3.3, 1405^{b}1, as an example of the proportional metaphor in which the metaphorical term supplies the lack of a proper term—"welding" for this special kind of application which was without a special name. He there proceeds to recommend riddles as a good source of metaphors, since "metaphor is a kind of enigma."

4. Probably meaning Homer.

5. I.e., in "lengthened" words. Below it is said that he could have burlesqued metaphors, foreign words, etc., in the same way. Eucleides has not been identified.

6. In the first line ("I saw Epichares walking to Marathon"), two short syllables must be arbitrarily lengthened to make a hexameter; and in the second line perhaps three short syllables must be so treated, but this line is textually corrupt,

and one can only make out "would not, in love(?) ... that man's hellebore."
Hellebore was a sedative recommended as a cure for madness.

7. "The gnawing ulcer that *eats* the flesh of my foot." Neither Aeschylus' play
nor that of Euripides has survived. The example has a certain irony, since Aeschylus was notorious for his use of strange words, and Euripides for his skillful
combination of current words (see note 12, below).

8. *Odyssey* 9.515, the Cyclops describing Odysseus: "But now a paltry man, a
weakling, in aspect ill-favored (has blinded me)."

9. Perhaps, "But now a little man, a man who is weak and unpleasing."

10. *Odyssey* 20.259, "Having placed (for him) an unseemly stool and a paltry
table," altered to "a wretched stool and a little table."

11. *Iliad* 17.265.

12. Unknown to us; he may have been a comic poet.

13. "Used in prose." It is uncertain whether the word *logoi* here means prose
or speeches or conversation, but this makes little difference since in *Rhetoric* 3.2,
1404^b31, we are told that "the current word, the distinctive word, and metaphor
alone are useful for the style of prose discourse (= oratory), ... for everyone uses
metaphors, distinctive words, and current words in conversation." Though in
this part of the *Rhetoric*, Aristotle is interested in distinguishing between the
poetical and rhetorical styles, he notes that the tragic poets of his day "have
discarded all those words, not in idiomatic use, which the early poets employed
for ornament, and which even today are so employed by the writers of hexameter verse" (1404^a29). It was Euripides who "led the way" to this natural style
in tragedy (1404^b25).

23. EPIC POETRY

1. In introducing the subject of Epic Poetry, Aristotle proceeds in a way that
recalls his introduction of Tragedy (Chapter 6); he places the type as to manner
and medium; assumes that the objects are men in action and insists on the need
for unity established in Chapter 7; and he touches, as in the case of Tragedy, on
the *ergon*, or characteristic effect of the form. On the last point, he has left it to
his critics to raise the question whether the proper "pleasure" *(hêdonê)* of Epic
Poetry is the same as that of Tragedy. The end of Chapter 26, however, implies
that they are the same.

2. On the same day, according to Herodotus 7.166.

3. Cf. Chapter 8, 1451^a19–22. The words "might seem divine *(thespesios)*"
perhaps allude to the common descriptions of Homer as "divine" *(theios)*.

4. *Iliad* 2.484 ff.

5. The *Cypria* and the *Little Iliad* were post-Homeric poems, completing the
Epic Cycle by describing the events of the Trojan War preceding and following
the events of the *Iliad*, the *Cypria* apparently beginning with the Judgment of
Paris and ending with the arrival of the Greeks before Troy, and the *Little Iliad*
beginning with the contest for Achilles' arms and ending with the departure of
the Greeks. They seem to have had little inner structure. The *Cypria* was often
ascribed to Stasinus of Cyprus and the *Little Iliad* to Lesches of Mitylene.

6. This list appears to have undergone some alteration. "More than eight" is
an odd way of saying "ten," and in fact the first eight themes follow the order of

events in the *Little Iliad*, according to our information about the poem, while the last two probably belong to another lost epic, *The Sack of Troy*. If the last two were added here, perhaps as an afterthought by Aristotle himself, "eight" may have been hastily altered to "more than eight." "Tragedies" in this passage does not mean individual plays—there might be many plays entitled *Philoctetes*—but tragic actions; cf. above, Chapter 18, 1456ª7, and note.

24. EPIC POETRY (CONTINUED)

1. See Chapter 18, 1455ᵇ32. "Should include"—Aristotle instinctively thinks of tragedy as in nature prior to epic poetry and "followed" by it (Chapter 5, 1449ᵇ10). In this paragraph, references to the six constituent elements (from which, however, Character is omitted) seem to have been superimposed on a straightforward statement about the four varieties as illustrated by Homer (Friedrich Solmsen, "The Origins and Methods of Aristotle's *Poetics*." *CQ* 29 [1935], 194-195).

2. The *Iliad* is designated as a poem of passion and the *Odyssey* as a poem of character in the same way as tragedies are so described in Chapter 18 (see note 3). The action of the *Iliad* turns upon the passionate character of Achilles, that of the *Odyssey* upon the human and flexible character of Odysseus; the *Iliad* accordingly presents a succession of scenes of suffering, the *Odyssey* a succession of ethical scenes. The first word of the *Iliad* is "wrath," of the *Odyssey* "man."

3. Chapter 7.

4. In Aristotle's time, this would probably be three tragedies, and if these equaled in length the fifth-century tragedies known to us, the total length would be roughly 5,000 lines or less (but the reduction of the choral parts to intercalary songs is hard to reckon with). The *Iliad* as we have it contains 15,693 lines, the *Odyssey* 12,105. After Aristotle, though probably not under his influence, the *Argonautica* of Apollonius Rhodius has 5,385 lines, Virgil's *Aeneid* 9,896.

5. It is convenient to translate *epi tês skênês* as "on the stage" (also Chapter 17, 1455ª28), and indeed the Theater of Dionysus may already have had a low stage in Aristotle's time; but the words literally mean "at" or "before the *skênê*"—i.e., the painted building behind the orchestra. See A. Pickard-Cambridge, *The Theatre of Dionysus* (Oxford, 1946), p. 73.

6. In the *Odyssey*, all that happens to Telemachus at Pylos and Sparta is contemporaneous with all that happens to Odysseus in Phaeacia, until father and son arrive at the same time in Ithaca. Actually, this treatment of time is rare in Homer, and, as the next sentence shows, Aristotle seems mostly to be thinking of "episodes" (= "parts") in a looser sense, perhaps even of the Catalogue of Ships: Homer took only a "part" of the war as his subject in the *Iliad*, and brought in many other parts as episodes (1459ª35); the core action of the *Odyssey* may be briefly stated, "and all the rest is episodes" (1455ᵇ23).

The present passage may have lent support to the neoclassical rule of the Unity of Place, but Castelvetro, the real author of the Three Unities, seems to have deduced unity of the place on rational grounds without reliance on Aristotle; see Allan H. Gilbert, *Literary Criticism, Plato to Dryden*, (Philadelphia: Richard West, 1978), p. 105, n. 153.

7. The meaning is that plays imitating the same action (play after play repre-

senting the fall of Oedipus, for example) are almost obliged to use the same episodes over and over again *ad nauseam*; but the freedom of epic makes it possible, theoretically at least, to compose another *Iliad* or *Odyssey*, using quite different episodes from those used by Homer.

8. Reading ταύτῃ *(tautêi)* with Twining. According to Chapter 22 (1459ª10), foreign words befit epic and metaphors dramatic dialogue; it is thought that in the present passage Aristotle may refer to the Homeric simile, since he regards the simile as a form of metaphor (*Rhet.* 3.4, 1406ᵇ20).

9. Compare Chapter 4, 1449ª24.

10. E.g., a god or a goddess. Note that here "imitation" is narrowed to mean "impersonation," the meaning it regularly has in Plato.

11. *Iliad* 22.205 ff. Achilles shakes his head at his men to restrain them from shooting Hector down and thus spoiling his own impending victory.

12. False inference, the so-called "fallacia consequentis"; cf. Aristotle, *Sophistic Refutations* 5, 167ᵇ1 ff. See the earlier example in Chapter 16, 1455ª13. This topic still falls under the head of the irrational in epic poetry, but it is rather irrationally introduced here, since it is not an improbability in the poet's narrative.

13. I.e. *Odyssey* 19.165-260; the Homeric poems had not yet been divided into books in Aristotle's time. Odysseus, disguised as a beggar, pretends that he is a Cretan who in better days had entertained Odysseus in Crete. He correctly describes Odysseus' dress and ornaments and his squire Eurybates. Penelope knows that the description is true and hence wrongly accepts as true the lie to which it is "added."

14. So mandatory is the principle of probability that in a crucial instance the poet should reject an incredible incident even if the thing is possible and should choose the probable incident even if it is really impossible, since in this case the impossible, being probable, will not be dramatically irrational; at all costs one should avoid having irrational parts in one's plots. We have just been told that epic narrative offers more scope for the irrational than does tragedy; but the dramatic plot is the norm for epic as well, and the thought must now be completed with the warning that, though there may be irrational details, the plot structure should not depend on them and where they are present they should be concealed. Probability is all. This seems to acknowledge the principle of dramatic illusion; the action of *Oedipus Tyrannus* very likely is impossible, but Sophocles has manipulated it so that his plot seems probable.

15. In Sophocles' *Oedipus Tyrannus*, it is incredible that Oedipus, as king of Thebes, should not have heard how his predecessor met his death, but Sophocles suppresses this irrational element of his plot. In the same poet's *Electra* 680-760, the false report of Orestes' death at the Pythian Games was criticized in antiquity as an anachronism, since the Pythian Games had not yet been founded in the time of Orestes. Sophocles' *Mysians* is lost, but is probably the play referred to here, though tragedies with this title are recorded also for Aeschylus, Nicomachus, Agathon, and (doubtfully) Euripides. The story is that of Telephus (Chapter 13, 1453ª21). Having slain his uncle in Tegea in Arcadia, he was sent by the oracle to Mysia in Asia Minor to be cleansed of his blood guilt, being meanwhile under a ban of silence; in Mysia he was saved from marrying his unknown mother by a timely Recognition. His silence, presumably in this play, was no-

torious and a source of humorous allusion in the comedies of Aristotle's time—e.g., in the *Parasites* of Alexis (frg. 178): "Telephus dines without uttering a word, just nodding his head at the people who ask him questions." This may be the very scene Aristotle alludes to.

16. *Odyssey* 13.166 ff. Odysseus sleeps throughout the voyage from Phaeacia, and fails to awaken even when the Phaeacians run the ship aground in Ithaca, put him ashore with his many possessions, and take their departure.

17. In epic poetry, the less vital (literally "the idle") parts perhaps are those in which the poet speaks in his own person—i.e., the undramatic parts. If, in the preceding sentence, the words "the other good features" refer to style, consideration of the Landing Scene may have suggested the present reflection.

25. CRITICAL PROBLEMS AND THEIR SOLUTIONS

1. This interesting and well-arranged chapter is in place here, since its illustrations are drawn from epic poetry (Homer), though its principles apply also to drama, and it leads easily into the final critical problem (Chapter 26) of the relative worth of epic and tragedy. It sets out to discover the number and nature of the kinds of critical problems and their solutions; first lays down some basic assumptions; then exhibits a number of concrete solutions (or answers to critical objections); gives two examples of general method; abstracts from the listed solutions the general nature of the problems; and concludes that there are five classes of problems, illustrated in twelve solutions. The procedure is efficient; the selected problems are presented as attacks on the poet and the solutions as defense, so that the whole has the appearance of a defense of the poet, though not of the received text. The method is inductive; the five general problems are abstracted from the preceding concrete solutions, which are not put down under these five heads but merely divided into solutions relating to "the art" and solutions relating to "language." The content and the orderly arrangement of the chapter suggest that it bore a close relationship to Aristotle's book *Homeric Problems*, which is lost but is known to us from citations in the ancient commentaries on Homer. The chapter also has some relation to Aristotle's treatise *On Sophistic Refutations*, in which some of the same examples are found.

2. Poetry is an autonomous art; incorrectness in handling the matter of some other art, if this serves the poet's purpose, is not an artistic fault, though all mistakes should if possible be avoided. Plato, too, thought that such incorrectness was inherent in imitative poetry, and on that account he condemns the art as untruthful (*Rep.* 10, 600E-602B; *Laws* 2, 667B-669A; *Ion* 537A). Aristotle is not answering him in reaffirming that such "untruthfulness" may indeed be demanded by the art. Plato himself knew that poetry is autonomous: "The poet is obliged to know scales and rhythm [i.e., his own art] but is by no means obliged to know whether his imitations are good or not good" (sc. morally); *Laws* 2, 670E. The latter knowledge belongs to the political art, not to the art of poetry. The political art can neither compose poetry nor reform it, but can judge it. If poetry could be reformed, Plato would have admonished the poets and not driven them away.

3. Some words have been lost from the Greek text at this point. The restoration is by Vahlen.

4. That horses may actually assume this gait was unknown to Aristotle, who believed that with such a movement a horse would lose its balance and fall over (*On the Progression of Animals* 712ª24). The example seems to suit painting or sculpture more naturally than poetry.

5. The Greek text adds: "or (if) impossibilities have been represented."

6. The criticisms and solutions are arranged in two groups, those relating to the essential art of imitation and those relating to language. Six criticisms, usually marked off by a transitional phrase, are examined in each of the two groups, making twelve in all, as stated at the end of the chapter. In much the same way, in his *Sophistic Refutations* 4-5, Aristotle divides fallacies between those depending upon language and those depending on logic.

7. Chapter 24, 1460ª15. There the Pursuit was classified as "irrational" (or "improbable"), here it seems less well placed under the "impossible," but these categories are very similar; the subject matter of poetry (Chapter 9, 1450ᵇ38) is "things possible, as being probable or necessary."

8. E.g., in the case of the Pursuit, it is the art of generalship. Cf. Plato, *Ion* 537A ff.

9. Pindar, *Olympian* 3.29, has "a female deer with golden horns," and the scholiast notes that the error was common among poets and artists.

10. Sophocles' comment is known only from this passage.

11. Xenophanes of Colophon, the early philosopher-poet (latter part of the sixth century B.C.), scorned anthropomorphism in general (frgs. 14-16) and censured Homer and Hesiod because they "attributed to the gods everything that among men is regarded as shameful and a reproach—theft, adultery, and deception of one another." (frg. 11 Diels). This clearly was not the "better" way of speaking of the gods; and as for the truth, the same Xenophanes says (frg. 34 Diels) that "no man has had or ever will have clear knowledge about the gods," only conjecture.

12. *Iliad* 10.152. The spears were so placed for the night while the encampment slept. Critics objected that they might fall down and cause alarm—i.e., the passage involved a mistake about "generalship," a special art. Aristotle (frg. 160) also dealt with this criticism of his *Homeric Problems*, giving the same solution as here.

13. *Iliad* 1.50. The pestilence sent by Apollo "attacked first the mules and the swift dogs." Aristotle alludes to the solution that took *oureus* (mule) as a foreign word for *ouros* (sentinel), the usual word for "mule" being *hêmionos* (Eustathius, *Commentary on Homer*).

14. *Iliad* 10.316.

15. *Iliad* 9.202. The Greeks drank wine mixed with water, and the less water the stronger the drink. The context of the Homeric passage seems to ensure that *zôroteros* means "stronger" or "purer," but the word itself was unknown to the critics, and Plutarch devotes a long chapter of his *Convivial Questions* (5.4) to the attempts made to explain it. The criticism falls under moral problems, and the solution under "foreign" words. Empedocles apparently assumed that *zôroteros* was the comparative of a word *zôros* meaning "pure" (below, 1461ª25).

16. *Iliad* 10.1-2, 11-15; but partly confused with *Iliad* 2.1-2.

17. *Iliad* 18.489; *Od.* 5.275: "She alone is without a share in the baths of

Ocean"—i.e., the constellation of the Great Bear does not set. But this is true of all the northern constellations, not merely of the Great Bear.

18. These words were read in Aristotle's time at *Iliad* 2.15, but are absent from our texts. The difficulty is that if Zeus bids the false Dream to tell Agamemnon "we grant him the fulfilment of his prayer," it is a falsehood, since Zeus did not fulfil it. Hippias changed the accent from *dídomen*, "we grant," to *didómen* (=imperative), "grant," and thus made the Dream and not Zeus responsible for deceiving Agamemnon. Hippias of Thasos has not been identified.

19. *Iliad* 23.327. "A part of which *(hou)* rots in the rain" (of a stump of oak or pine used as a goal post); but perhaps because this point would be irrelevant, Hippias altered *hou* to *ou*, "which does *not* rot in the rain," and this is what our texts of Homer read. These two solutions by accent also appear in *Sophistic Refutations* 4, 166^{b}2-9, in less abbreviated form.

20. Empedocles, fragment 35, vv. 14–15 Diels. A comma is to be placed after the second "before." The subject is the four elements, which are in themselves indestructible, but combine to form a destructible world.

21. The explanation here added in brackets is not certain. The passage is *Iliad* 10.252.

22. *Iliad* 21.592. Tin seems an absurd material for armor; but the word is explained analogously as standing for the mixture of tin and copper—i.e., bronze.

23. *Iliad* 20.234. The gods drink nectar. Note the chiastic order: wine mixture = tin mixture (bronze) while the abusive application of "bronze" (brazier) = the abusive application of "wine" (wine pourer).

24. *Iliad* 20.268-72. The spear thrown by Aeneas struck the divine shield of Achilles made of five layers of metal: "but it failed to break the shield, for the gold restrained it, the gift of the god; but it passed through two layers, and there were still three more, since the lame god had made five layers in all, two of bronze and two, inside, of tin and this one of gold—*there the ashen spear was stopped.*" If it was stopped at the golden layer, which presumably was outside, how could it have passed through two layers? This problem the ancient commentators sensibly solved by assuming that "was stopped" meant that its impetus was checked by the outer layer, but enough force still remained to carry it though this (golden) layer and the first bronze layer. This solution may well have been in Aristotle's mind when he altered the original verb to one meaning "check" or "hinder," but he does not propose this or any other solution here, as he has done in the earlier cases. This is not a thirteenth Solution, but an example of method.

25. Perhaps to be identified with the Glaucon favorably mentioned as an interpreter of Homer by Plato, *Ion* 530D.

26. Icarius was the father of Penelope and hence Telemachus's grandfather. Homer tells us nothing about him except his name, but ancient critics identified him with Icarius the brother of Spartan Tyndareus, and thus created the problem here mentioned (cf. Porphyry on *Od.* 4.1, and scholia on *Od.* 1.285 and 2.52).

27. The difference of only one letter between Icarius and Icadius shows us that we are in the realm of textual correction. To be sure, a textual correction affecting a good number of passages—for the name Icarius occurs sixteen times

in the *Odyssey*, though nearly always in the formula "daughter of Icarius"—may seem to us hard to justify. But apparently it would not seem so to Aristotle, if, as we are informed (frg. 171 Rose), he elsewhere emended *audêessa* to *aulêessa* (also a change of a single letter), or to *oudêessa*, in some five places in the *Odyssey*. Such an error might well seem possible to him in the transmission of the text by rhapsodes. To understand the last phrase as "a mistake of the critics" (Bywater, Lucas) ignores Icarius/Icadius, which is the point of what the Cephalonians said; and to impute the mistake to Homer (Rostagni) stultifies Aristotle's point.

28. Chapter 24, 1460ᵃ26.

29. Chapter 18, 1456ᵃ24.

30. The method is expressed as a formula, which would be enough to convey the sense to Aristotle's auditors. In a debate you must watch your opponent's rebuttal to make sure that he has not shifted the meaning of your words, or disregarded their special relevance, or used them in a sense you did not mean. See Aristotle, *Sophistic Refutations*, Chapter 5, 167ᵃ21–37.

31. This sentence seems only to restate on the frame of dialectical method the advice already given (1461ᵃ31) to try out all the possible meanings of a seemingly contradictory expression, and the implication is that endeavor on these lines will lead to a Solution. In fact, the examples in the first language solution (No. 7) were perhaps chosen to illustrate the point. The poet is defended as meaning by *ourêas the same thing* as a sensible reader assumes when he sees that it means not "mules" but "sentinels"; *eidos* must be meant *in relation to* face only, not the whole body; and *zôoteron* is not used *in the sense* of "stronger" but of "faster." But the rule applies in one way or another to all the language problems.

32. In Euripides' *Medea* 663 ff., the sudden arrival of Aegeus is unmotivated and hence perhaps improbable; his function is to fortify Medea with the assurance of a refuge, but this may have seemed to Aristotle unnecessary, since Medea can rely on supernatural resources of her own.

33. Cf. Chapter 15, 1454ᵃ29.

26. WHICH IS BETTER—EPIC POETRY OR TRAGEDY?

1. Such a comparison would be meaningless if Aristotle did not think that the two forms have the same object—the arousal of pity and fear. See the end of the chapter.

2. Probably an allusion to Timotheus' dithyramb *Scylla*, mentioned in Chapter 15 (1454ᵃ31). In the *Odyssey* (12.245–59), the sea monster Scylla seizes six of Odysseus' men from the ship and devours them.

3. I.e., epic poetry is the older as well as the more dignified form. Mynniscus appeared in the later plays of Aeschylus, presumably as a young man, since he was still acting in 422 B.C. Callipides was active in the last two decades of the fifth century, and is mentioned in the biography of Sophocles; he boasted of his ability to reduce the audience to tears (Xenophon, *Symposium* 3, 11). Pindarus is mentioned only here.

4. The audience presumably is the same, but made up partly of educated persons and partly of the vulgar sort; tragedy, it is alleged, aims to please the

vulgar, while epic recitations are directed toward the better class. Aristotle has himself deplored the fact that the poets yield to the taste of the audience, which prefers happy endings (Chapter 13, 1153ª33). In the case of musical contests, he seems to contemplate separating the popular audience from the educated (*Politics* 8, 7, 1342ª18-28): "Since the audience is of a dual nature, an audience of freemen and educated persons, and a vulgar audience made up of mechanics and laborers and the like, there ought to be competitions and shows to furnish relaxation for people of this kind also. Just as their souls are warped from the natural state, so also violent and chromatic tunes are deviations from the normal scales; and, therefore, since each type of person enjoys what is naturally suited to it, performers before an audience of this kind ought to be permitted to employ this kind of music." Plato, from a similar point of view, gives the preference to epic (*Laws* 658D); "Young boys would give the prize to comedy; educated women, young men, *and perhaps the majority of the audience* would vote for tragedy; but we older men would take most pleasure in listening to a rhapsode giving a fine recitation of the *Iliad* or the *Odyssey* or a poem of Hesiod, and would declare him definitely the winner." See also Plato's *Gorgias* 501-502 on the aim of tragedy to please the crowd.

5. Sosistratus and Mnasitheus are unknown; the first evidently was a rhapsode like Plato's *Ion*, the second presumably a citharoedus, who sang to his own accompaniment on the cithara.

6. The ancients seem generally to have read aloud even when alone. Cf. Chapter 14, 1453ᵇ4-7 on the satisfactory effect of merely hearing a tragedy without seeing it played.

7. Since tragedy has its proper effect when merely read, the movement of actors (= stage presentation) is not a necessary part of it; for if the absence of something makes no difference, that thing is not part of the whole (1451ª34). In thus discounting "movement," Aristotle disposes of the charge of vulgarity, and some commentators think "this" should be understood as "this objection" or "this defect" (i.e., vulgarity), but the nearer reference to "movement" seems more likely. How Spectacle can be "necessarily" a part of tragedy (1449ᵇ31), and yet, as the activity of actors, "not necessarily" a part of it, is explained at the end of Chapter 6 (1450ᵇ16-20).

8. In the surviving Greek plays, the hexameter is very rarely used, but, as Piero Pucci has pointed out to me, where it is used—e.g., in Sophocles' *Trachiniae* 1010-22 and Euripides' *Suppliants* 271-4, 282-5—it produces a strong emotional effect as a "departure from the tonality of normal speech" (Chapter 4, 1449ª27).

9. After "music" the MSS. add "and spectacle," destroying the grammar of the Greek sentence. Spectacle is indeed an advantage that tragedy has over epic, but Aristotle may not have cared to say so here, since he has just discounted its effect and recommended reading. Music is more internal, since it primarily means the choral odes.

10. Tragedy and epic poetry are two instruments designed to do the same work (to arouse pity and fear in the reader or spectator), and tragedy does it better. That pity and fear are not mentioned in the discussion of epic poetry in Chapters 23 and 24 need cause no surprise; the discussion of epic is a mere annex to the discussion of tragedy, noting some peculiarities of epic and assuming that

the principles of tragedy apply to it. Indeed, it may be inferred from Chapter 4 that Aristotle regards epic poetry as an undeveloped form of tragedy, perhaps even that the form of tragedy pre-existed and that Homer and the early dramatists caught increasingly adequate glimpses of it.

11. A summary formulation of this kind is commonly used by Aristotle as a transition to a new topic, and here the expected sequel would be the discussion of Comedy promised in Chapter 6. Promises are not always kept, but perhaps there is sufficient evidence to show that a second book of the *Poetics*, on comedy, once existed and has been lost. Most significant are two references by Aristotle himself in the *Rhetoric* to a treatment of the comic in the *Poetics*—"the subject of the laughable has been separately discussed in the *Poetics*" (*Rhet.* 1.11, 1371^{b}36) and "the forms of the laughable have been enumerated in the *Poetics*" (*Rhet.* 3.18, 1419^{b}6). The most reliable of the ancient lists of Aristotle's works gives the *Pragmateia*, usually identified with our *Poetics*, as in two books, and there are two late references to our *Poetics* as Book I (see the critical notes in Kassel's ed., p. 49). An anonymous tract *On Comedy* (the *Tractatus Coislinianus*) has sometimes been thought to reflect Aristotle's doctrine on this subject. For the contrary view, that no second book on comedy ever existed, see I. Düring, *Aristoteles* (Heidelberg, 1966), p. 126.

- The idea of universality of poetry make possible the emphasis on plot rather than character.

- The universality is what makes possible mimesis as didactic tool.